CHILDREN AND DIVORCE

The Practice of Social Work

General editors: Bill Jordan and Jean Packman

1 MATE AND STALEMATE
Janet Mattinson and Ian Sinclair

2 GROWING UP IN CARE
Ten People Talking
Barbara Kahan

3 CREATIVE SOCIAL WORK
David Brandon and Bill Jordan (editors)

4 CHILDREN, GRIEF AND SOCIAL WORK
Gill Lonsdale, Peter Elfer and Rod Ballard

5 OCCUPATIONAL SURVIVAL
The Case of the Local Authority Social Worker
Carole Satyamurti

6 CHILDREN AND DIVORCE
Martin Wilkinson

7 A PLACE CALLED HOPE
Caring for Children in Distress
Tom O'Neill

8 KIDS AT THE DOOR
A Preventive Project on a Council Estate
Bob Holman

9 A BRIDGE TO INDEPENDENCE
The Kent Family Placement Project
Nancy Hazel

Children and Divorce

MARTIN WILKINSON

Basil Blackwell · Oxford

First published in 1981 by
Basil Blackwell Publisher
108 Cowley Road
Oxford OX4 1JF
England

The persons referred to in the case material in this book are fictional. The characters have been created to illustrate as realistically as possible some of the more typical situations with which a court welfare officer may be faced. They do not represent the actual circumstances of any divorced couples or of their children in real life.

British Library Cataloguing in Publication Data
Wilkinson, Martin
Children and divorce. – (The practice of social work).
1. Family social work
I. Title II. Series
362.82 HQ10

ISBN 0-631-12514-0
ISBN 0-631-12524-8 Pbk

Typeset in IBM Press Roman by Freeman Graphic, Tonbridge
Printed and Bound in Great Britain by Book Plan Ltd, Worcester

Contents

Acknowledgements

My thanks are due to Michael Day, Chief Probation Officer, and the Committee of the West Midlands Probation and After-Care Service, for allowing me leave of absence in which to write this book. I also wish to thank the Barrow & Geraldine S. Cadbury Trust, without whose generous financial assistance the undertaking would not have been possible.

I am indebted to Dr Jean Packman for her encouragement and her sympathetic advice as Editor, and also to Drs Denis and Barbara Gray of the Department of Extra Mural Studies of Birmingham University and Donald Hamilton, Barrister, who have given their time to read the manuscript. They have all made many helpful comments and suggestions, and their contributions have been much valued. They do not, of course, bear any responsibility for such errors as I may have succeeded in introducing despite their vigilance.

It is not possible to acknowledge individually the help and encouragement that I have received from many colleagues. Particular thanks are due, however, to Anne Wedgwood-Oppenheim, for her assistance in checking the manuscript and preparing the index; to Judy Tolley and Pam Waterhouse, for much typing and secretarial help; and not least to my wife and family, for their forbearance whilst the work has been in progress.

FOR VIVIEN

1

Divorce and the Welfare Service

The dramatic rise in the rate of divorce in this country has been one of the major social phenomena of the past 30 years. The explanations advanced for it have been many and complex. They have included the radical change in the status of women; the decline in formal religious observance; and the heightened expectation of happiness and fulfilment in personal relationships. Where these relationships have been formalized by marriage, they have come to be viewed increasingly as legal and terminable contracts rather than as unions which are by definition immutable. All these factors contributed to a climate of opinion which made it possible to liberalize the law of divorce. The culmination was the Divorce Reform Act of 1969, which brought the dissolution of marriage effectively within the reach of all for the first time.

Easier divorce should not, however, be equated automatically with less painful divorce. It remains an acutely traumatic experience both for the parties themselves and for their children. The need to mitigate its damaging consequences at a personal level has gradually come to be more appreciated and its very prevalence has helped it to secure some greater measure of social acceptability. Nowhere has the concern been greater than for the children who are its victims and the provision for their protection has been progressively extended and refined.

The development of the court's own welfare arm under the aegis of the Probation and After-Care Service has been one practical manifestation of that concern. It was envisaged initially as an investigative service, with a duty to report to the court in matters affecting the welfare of children in divorce proceedings. It was also given a supervisory function in respect of those children for whom some external oversight was considered necessary. Recognition of the value of attempting to conciliate between parties and of supporting them in their separate parenting roles after divorce has led to its subsequent development as a counselling service. It is now as much engaged in fostering positive relationships between parents and between parents and their children when marriages end as it is in helping to resolve the purely legal aspects of custody and access disputes.

AN HISTORICAL RESUME

The emergent welfare service can best be placed in its historical and social context by touching, albeit very cursorily, upon the principal landmarks in the development of divorce legislation in this country, with particular emphasis upon the provision made for the care and welfare of children.

The Civil Law of Divorce

Divorce was first brought within the ambit of the civil courts by the Matrimonial Causes Act of 1857. Prior to this, jurisdiction in matrimonial issues had rested exclusively with the ecclesiastical courts, apart from the right (which was very seldom exercised) to petition directly to Parliament by means of a private Bill for the dissolution of an individual marriage. The provisions of the Act were limited and discriminatory, for whilst a husband could petition on the grounds of a single act of adultery, a wife had also to adduce additional misconduct such as desertion, cruelty or sexual malpractice. Primitive as this may now seem as divorce law, some provision was nonetheless made from the outset for the children. The Act empowered the court to make such order 'as it may deem just and proper for the custody, maintenance and education of the children'.

The Matrimonial Causes Act of 1923 provided wives with the reciprocal right to petition on the grounds of simple adultery and a further Act in 1937 extended the grounds for divorce to include cruelty, desertion and incurable unsoundness of mind. The fundamental criterion for determining custody issues had meanwhile been introduced with the Guardianship of Infants Act of 1925, which established the welfare of the child as the first and paramount consideration.

A Private Member's Bill in 1951 proposed a radical reform in the law of divorce. In allowing either party to petition on the grounds of a seven-year separation, it would have breached significantly the traditional concept of innocent and guilty parties. The Bill was withdrawn on the appointment of a Royal Commission and the proposal was for the time being lost. The Act which followed the Commission's Report was, however, still of major importance because of the new provisions made for the welfare of children in divorce proceedings.

The Matrimonial Proceedings (Children) Act, 1958

This Act extended the definition of a child of the family in divorce proceedings to include those children of one party, whether of a previous marriage, adopted, or illegitimate, who have been accepted by the other partner as members of the family. It introduced a new form of protection by requiring that the judge declare himself satisfied as to the arrangements made for the care and upbringing of any children of the family before a decree nisi could be made absolute. It also provided for children to be placed under supervision or committed to the care of a local authority.

The term 'welfare officer' appeared for the first time in this Act and it was specified that the welfare officer should be a probation officer.

The Divorce Reform Act, 1969

This Act, now consolidated in the Matrimonial Causes Act 1973, provided the basis for the present law of divorce by introducing the principle of irretrievable breakdown of marriage as the sole ground for divorce. The Act requires that one or more of five conditions must be satisfied before a marriage can be held to be irretrievably broken down. They are that the respondent has committed adultery and the petitioner finds it intolerable to live with the respondent; that the respondent has behaved in such a way that the petitioner cannot reasonably be expected to live with the respondent; that the respondent has deserted the petitioner for a continuous period of at least two years; that the parties have lived apart for a continuous period of at least two years and the respondent consents to the divorce; or that the parties have lived apart for a continuous period of at least five years. The first three criteria do look suspiciously like their former parallel matrimonial offences, but the court is not required to find that the conduct complained of has actually caused the breakdown of the marriage. It is the fact of the breakdown that matters, rather than the attribution of blame for it; in theory at least, there are no longer innocent and guilty parties.

The provisions for the protection and welfare of children remained and still remain essentially the same as in the Act of 1958. There is the same requirement as to satisfaction and the same power to make care and supervision orders. The authority to make orders for custody (and by extension for access) still survives but little changed from the original Act of 1857. The court may, under the Act of 1973, make 'such order as it thinks fit for the custody and education of any child of the family who is under the age of eighteen'. The Rules (currently the Matrimonial Causes Rules, 1977) similarly provide for a judge or registrar to refer to a court welfare officer for investigation and report any matter in matrimonial proceedings which concerns the welfare of a child.

The introduction of divorce by consent and, subject to certain safeguards, of divorce on the grounds of separation alone without consent, was intended to facilitate the termination by law of marriages which had ceased to have any substance in anything other than a formal legal sense. The final removal of the traditional bars of connivance, collusion and condonation was another facet of this essentially pragmatic approach. The provision designed to foster reconciliation, on the other hand, has proved in the event to be almost wholly ineffective, so that the whole tenor has been towards easier, faster and less complicated divorce.

THE GROWTH OF THE WELFARE SERVICE

The initial impact on the Probation and After-Care Service of the new legislation of 1958 was comparatively slight. In 1960, when nearly 24,000 decrees of divorce were made absolute, only 880 welfare reports were called for. Statistics are not available as to the proportion of these divorces where there were children of the family or as to the actual number of children involved, but it is still clear that the use made by the courts of the welfare service was decidedly limited.

In 1970, some 58,000 decrees were made absolute. Nearly 36,000 of these marriages had relevant children, of whom there were over 71,000. The number of welfare enquiries had increased dramatically to over 6,200 – a rise in round figures from one report in every 27 divorces to one in every nine, with one in every six where children were concerned.

In 1977, by which time the divorce rate had again more than doubled, a similar pattern can be distinguished. The number of decrees made absolute was 129,000 involving nearly 149,000 children in some 77,500 families. The number of welfare reports called for had by then risen to almost 14,500, or approximately one in every five cases where there were relevant children.

These statistics must be treated with some caution. They do not, for example, differentiate between reports for satisfaction and those prepared in contested issues, where the divorce itself may have taken place some years earlier. Neither is any account taken of those cases in which welfare reports are prepared but the cause does not proceed to the making of a decree absolute. But despite these limitations it is still possible to discern a general trend: the courts have without question come to make an increasing demand upon the Welfare Service in relative as well as absolute terms over the course of the last decade.

THE MODERN CONCEPTION OF THE WELFARE SERVICE

Of greater interest perhaps than the growth of the Welfare Service in a purely statistical sense has been its response in social work terms to the new demands made of it. It has evolved increasingly sophisticated techniques in its complex statutory duty of preparing reports for the courts, and especially in contested issues. It has also become much more aware of the skills required to support both parents and children through the trauma of divorce and more adept in the practice of them. These skills it has also begun to carry through to the field of matrimonial supervision. Central to this part of its work is the concept of conciliation, which seeks as far as may be possible to heal the emotional wounds of the marital breakdown, so that the parties may conduct their future dealings with one another with reasonable harmony.

It is with these complementary rather than mutually exclusive tasks of reporting and conciliating and with the specific social work skills that they each demand that the following chapters will principally be concerned.

2

Reporter and Conciliator: The Dual Role

The first aspect of the welfare officer's role is defined by Rule 95(1) of the Matrimonial Causes Rules 1977, which empowers a judge or registrar to refer to him 'for investigation and report' any matter in matrimonial proceedings which concerns the welfare of a child. The process of enquiry which precedes the report cannot, however, take place in a vacuum. The fact that the enquiry is taking place will in itself cause changes in parental attitudes and outlook and a whole range of perceptions are likely to be altered as a result of the contact with the welfare officer. Implicit in this capacity for change is the second aspect of the welfare officer's role, that of conciliator. The essence of his task here is to foster healthy changes of attitude in the parents, minimizing the areas of conflict between them and helping them where necessary to come to terms with the fact that their marriage has ended. The search for mutually acceptable solutions to such issues of custody and access as may be before the court is an integral part of this process of conciliation, as also will be the reduction as far as may be possible of the inevitable feelings of bitterness and hostility when such solutions cannot be found.

It is not possible in practice to determine where the role of reporter ends and that of conciliator begins. Parents will properly invest a great deal of emotional energy in an enquiry which they know may have a profound effect upon their children's future. Their attention will not and should not be narrowly focused upon the particular application before the court. Their feelings about the marriage, the former partner and the effect of the separation upon themselves and their children will offer insights which may be of considerable significance to the reporting officer. The attitudes which emerge may also be important in the context of conciliation and there may be issues that he will wish to pursue at the same time as his enquiry proceeds. Counselling may then result in modifications to those attitudes, which in their turn will influence the final balance of the completed report. The two processes of investigation and conciliation are thus inextricably interwoven and very largely interdependent.[1]

The skills required for the two roles are not identical, but they are closely related and they do overlap. Common to both is the need to understand the dynamics of marriage and of marital breakdown and equally relevant will be an understanding of social attitudes towards divorce and of its impact at a personal emotional level. The reporting function will hold some common ground with the familiar duty of reporting to other courts in other contexts, although there will also be significant differences. The concept of post-marital counselling is perhaps less well established; it is certainly less familiar than traditional counselling in subsisting marriages. Its skills are, however, essential to the welfare officer, because of the extent to which unresolved marital problems affect the issues of custody, and especially of access, in relation to which he will wish to conciliate as well as to report.

Before examining each of these roles in greater detail it is necessary to sketch in something of the background against which the welfare officer's task is carried out. Their relevance in both comparative and absolute terms can only be evaluated in relation to prevailing social attitudes to divorce in general and to its emotional implications and consequences at an individual level.

SOCIAL ATTITUDES TOWARDS DIVORCE

Social attitudes towards divorce are much less straightforward than might be anticipated in the light of the reforms of recent years. With the replacement of the matrimonial offence by the concept of irretrievable breakdown and the adoption of the criterion of one party finding it intolerable to live with the other, divorce has acquired a much more civilized face. The legal process has been purged of some of its more sordid and hypocritical aspects and the mechanics of dissolution have been progressively simplified to the point where no attendance at court is required for the hearing of undefended causes. Divorce is more easy technically and less publicly traumatic for the individual than it has ever been and it has inevitably become a great deal more common in consequence.

This evident legal progress has not, however, been matched by a parallel shift in public attitudes. Although the movement for the reform of the divorce laws was substantial and well supported, it may not have been as fully representative of public opinion at large as is commonly supposed. Whilst it is true that social attitudes towards divorce have mellowed appreciably, particularly during the last decade, the old connotations of taint persist to a surprising extent.

The Public View of Marriage

It is commonly stated that marriage as an institution has been under greater threat during the past two generations than at any time during its history. The constraints upon long and short term relationships unsanctioned by marriage have largely vanished and cohabitation without permanent or formal commitment has been accorded an acceptance and indeed a respectability that would have been unthinkable 30 years ago. The social and emotional emancipation of women, whose economic dependence had previously made a mockery of their political and legal equality, has advanced rapidly and has contributed substantially to the changing climate. Social and economic freedom is attainable by both sexes at an ever earlier age and some at least have been moved to seek an alternative to the permanent monogamous sexual relationship now that it has the very real potential to endure for upwards of 50 years.

Despite the various assaults upon it marriage has, perhaps against expectations, become more rather than less popular. It may be seen more as a contract between equals which is dissoluble by mutual consent and less as the life-long commitment it used to be, but it remains by far the most common and commonly desired arrangement between couples who live together. The well-publicized dissent of a vocal and articulate minority has had little impact upon public opinion and social attitudes still reflect the essential popularity of marriage. People are still expected to want to marry and those who do not do so are seen as being both unfulfilled and disadvantaged. Their single status still tends to be ascribed to want of opportunity rather than the exercise of individual choice, or sometimes to even darker motivations if the possibility of choice is conceded. For the great majority who do marry, there are fairly specific expectations in terms of their behaviour, expectations which, in the case of women at least, often persist even after their marriages are ended. To stray beyond the bounds of the conventionally accepted role is still to invite a very real measure of social disapproval.

Divorce and Bereavement: the Parallel Denial

Partir, c'est mourir un peu: the French observation is perceptive, for something within does indeed die when any significant relationship comes to an end. When the relationship is a marriage and it is ended by divorce the reaction can be as intense as that produced by an actual bereavement and it will in many ways be akin to it. The description of divorce as mourning without death gives some indication of the magnitude of the difficulties faced by those who suffer final marriage breakdown.

The parallel between divorce and bereavement is important, because the way in which society reacts to death may throw some light upon its responses to divorce. The way in which we as a society refuse to face up to the fact of death whilst we prepare with an ever-increasing sophistication for every other contingency in life is graphically described by Lily Pincus.[2] Despite our knowledge that we need to mourn our losses and that we do suffer both physically and psychologically when we are denied the opportunity to do so, we still fail, in her opinion, to create a climate in which mourning is accepted and acceptable. Her conclusion that 'the first therapeutic task in our society . . . is to give sanction to mourning' must be of major significance to all who work with the divorced.

The conspiracy of denial in death, damaging as it must be to the bereaved, at least contains none of the hypocrisy and double standards which are features of our uneasy response to divorce. A society which is denigrating in its attitudes towards those who choose not to marry must be expected to be even more punitive in its approach to those who fail to stay married. The concept of failing to stay married is important, because it carries by implication connotations of not having tried hard enough to save the marriage and therefore of being personally to blame for its breakdown. To legislate for the dissolution of manifestly unworkable marriages with as little pain and as much dignity as can be achieved may be acceptable in theory. In practice, however, those who need to obtain such dissolutions are still diminished in the eyes of society because they have been found wanting in the talents and the determination which make marriages survive. In blaming the individual for his failure, society also withdraws its approval and support. If it cannot bring itself to help those whose losses through death are not attributable to personal fault, it will have little sympathy to spare for those who it believes have contributed to their own disasters.

Society's wish to turn its face away from the unpleasant fact of divorce and the law's much more enlightened wish to detraumatize its necessary legal processes have colluded unconsciously, and to a degree unfortunately, in rendering it almost too impersonal and anonymous. Just as the ending of a relationship by death needs to be marked by the ritual of the funeral before mourning can begin its healing process, so too does the fact of divorce need to be marked by a similar terminating ritual. The ending of a major relationship, often of many years standing, without any ceremony and without any social acknowledgement of its importance to the individual can leave the newly divorced feeling bereft not only of support and approval but of any real sense of their new identity. This is well brought out in the following personal description, in which the parallel between divorce and bereavement is again a feature:

> Divorce, separation, desertion or death are events that require 'letting go' skills, especially when children are involved. From the time we're born we are taught how to say 'hello' but seldom if ever do we learn how to say 'goodbye'. I can clearly remember the day of my divorce and my anger that this 'letting go' process

> had none of the elements of my marriage ceremony. No one was there to celebrate the ending of a destructive relationship, or to advise me on my new state of single parenthood. There was little sign of community interest and no approval like the day of my marriage. There was no ritual to allow me, my children and my husband to let go gracefully. I remember thinking that if one of us had died, we would at least have received support in our grief.[3]

Divorce is shown here as something more than the dissolution of a legal contract and the need for it to be acknowledged as an emotional as well as a purely legal event is apparent. The need for it to be accorded some specific social recognition is also clear. It is at least possible that the pendulum has swung too far in favour of quick and 'painless' divorce and that some element of cathartic ritual should be introduced.

Sexual Discrimination: the Differential Status

It has taken women until comparatively recently to achieve a genuine measure of equality in marriage. They have, with the relative improvement in their economic status and the assistance of the reformed divorce law, also achieved a more nearly equal opportunity to divorce and the right to a more equitable division of the matrimonial possessions after that event. What they have yet to achieve as divorced women is an equal status with their former partners. Old prejudices die hard and they still tend in consequence to be stigmatized to an appreciably greater extent than divorced men.

There is no readily definable place in society for the divorced woman, who will frequently have the responsibility of caring for her children and who cannot revert to a single status with the same ease as her male counterpart. Social attitudes towards her remain equivocal for so long as she continues unattached. There is a greater expectation that she should continue to conduct herself as befits a married woman, regardless of the fact that she is divorced. She will, for example, be much less readily forgiven than her former husband should she seek the emotional and sexual satisfaction to which she may have become accustomed outside the confines of a new marital or quasi-marital relationship. Unjust as it may be, she continues to be regarded by too many of her still married sisters as a potential predator and to be devalued as at best a second hand future wife. She will be characterized with equally little justification by a proportion of her male acquaintances as holding the promise of a more easy promiscuity than can be expected of either married or single women. Deliberately exaggerated these stereotypes may be, but they do nonetheless contain a sufficient element of truth to make the lot of the divorced woman more lonely and more unhappy than it would otherwise be.

Divorced men do have their own peculiar problems. The decision to abandon a career in order to raise a family will often be met with a disapproval which would not be visited upon their wives in similar circumstances. Again, they have been guilty of ceasing to behave like conventionally married men and they are stigmatized by society for forcing it to acknowledge their change in status. When, by contrast, they have been relieved of or denied the responsibility of caring for their children and this is the case with the majority of divorced men – a curious double standard is applied as they revert to all outward appearances to a bachelor role. Their restored single status is more readily acceptable at its face value, with society apparently prepared to give its tacit approval to the situation so long as it is not forced openly to recognize it. They are usually seen as less of a threat to other marriages than are their former wives and any occasional sexual involvements are much less obviously frowned upon. The old dual standard of sexual morality still prevails and if the divorced man is not granted the licence to behave exactly as he chooses, he is at least assured of an appreciably greater level of general tolerance.

The principal reason for the differential status after divorce, apart from the dual standard of morality which the women's liberation movement has so far failed to break down, can be found in the continuing general practice of awarding the custody of children in divorce proceedings to the mother. It is true that fathers do now have a much more credible image as custodial parents than used to be the case, but their successful custody applications are still the exception rather than the rule. This fact by itself makes the lone mother a less marriageable prospect than her former husband. It does, however, have the additional effect of rendering her need for the support of a second partner all the more urgent. Any recognition of the problems which she faces as a single parent may cause her to be seen as a threat to existing marriages because of her evident need for a substitute father for her family. The defensive reaction which this produces is to cast her even more firmly in the acceptable and unthreatening role of mother only and to deny her as far as possible the status of potential wife. Thus even when she can overcome the obstacles inherent in her situation as a single parent, there are social forces at work which will seek to prevent her from escaping from that depressed and disadvantaged status.

THE EMOTIONAL CONSEQUENCES OF DIVORCE

Individual responses to divorce vary according to the personalities of the people involved and the circumstances surrounding the marriage breakdown. They will be conditioned in part by such considerations as who left whom, and why; what happened to the children and to the matrimonial home; and what social and professional supports were available and how effectively they were utilized. Within this broad framework there are certain characteristics which are common to most of the newly divorced. They include a low self-esteem; feelings of guilt, anger and ambivalence; concern for the children of the family; and the need, already touched upon, to sever the emotional as well as the legal bond of marriage.

The Damaged Self-Image

The most common emotional response to divorce is a deep sense of personal unworth. Society, as we have seen, attributes blame to those whose marriages do not survive and the sense of personal failure in the face of the collapse of this the most important of all adult relationships is all pervasive. The longer the relationship has lasted and the more that has been invested in it emotionally, the greater the trauma will be. It will have implications for the individual's self-image both as an adult personality in general and as a desirable sexual object in particular.

The adult personality

There is an element of regression in the reaction to the manifest rejection of divorce which is not unlike the child's response of 'I am unloved and therefore I am unlovable'. Since there is always the one who rejects as well as the one who is rejected there can also be the equally disturbing and guilt-inducing response of 'I cannot continue to love although I am still loved'. Few marriage breakdowns are the result of the total rejection by one partner of another who still loves totally. The elements are mixed in greater or lesser proportions, with each partner rejecting and being rejected, each feeling unable to love as well as feeling unloved.

Each of these reactions has its own connotation of personal failure and each can be carried over with crippling effect into the whole range of adult relationships which must perforce continue in some form after separation and divorce. This does not apply exclusively to heterosexual relationships, although it is here that the effect is likely to be most apparent. Sometimes the reaction will take the form of a deliberate avoidance of members of the opposite sex, declaring in effect that all of them have too great a capacity to hurt to be trusted again. Alternatively if the need to demonstrate an apparently undamaged survival is strong enough, it may result in a series of 'rebound' relationships. These can be dangerous, especially if one should progress as far as marriage with the objective still primarily one of obtaining personal reassurance rather than contributing to as well as taking from the new relationship.

The sexual image

The most obvious and direct damage to the sexual self-image occurs when one partner to the marriage is specifically rejected in favour of someone else. This is not, however, the only situation in which this kind of damage occurs. There is probably an element of it in every marriage breakdown, because the sense of having failed to hold on to one's partner will nearly always give rise to some doubts as to the capacity to continue to attract and to satisfy in a sexual sense. It can even apply to the partner who enters into the second relationship, if he or she is attempting to prove after one arid experience that the power of sexual attraction has not been destroyed.

The need for reassurance of continuing desirability in sexual terms can explain the apparently promiscuous and sometimes random sleeping around which on occasion follows a permanent separation. This behaviour may also contain elements of self-punishment which can almost amount to self-degradation, a putting to the proof, as it were, of the conviction of personal worthlessness.

The same need can also be identified in the almost desperate attempts of some still young women to demonstrate their continuing attractiveness. Their sense of style deserts them as, with make-up a little too emphatic and dresses a little too revealing or jeans a little too tight, their inappropriate efforts produce only a somewhat garish parody of the allure to which they aspire. It is in this type of situation that men can see an offer of actual availability which may be far from the truth and their wives a justification for the fears they entertain. The process is a sadly self-defeating one, in which the divorced wife remains the loser whether or not she manages to gain the attention which she is all too often ambivalent about attracting.

Anger, Guilt and Ambivalence

Anger, guilt and ambivalence are all commonly experienced feelings when a marriage breaks down. They are often so interwoven that it is difficult to separate out their individual strands. Anger against the former partner is readily understandable, but it can be directed inwardly as well. It can, for example, take the form of self-castigation in the prevailing mood of depression for not having been good enough to hold the marriage together. This can spill over into destructive self-recrimination as guilt prompts anxieties about the degree of personal responsibility for the breakdown. Ambivalence is almost always present, for few go into divorce without any regrets and without any backward glances to earlier and happier times. The questions will repeatedly present themselves:

how much choice was really left at the last and was the final step of divorce in truth unavoidable? Were such options as did remain open properly exercised? Should one perhaps have persisted longer or harder, or at least differently?

These tangled emotions all feed the fires of depression, self-doubt and personal devaluation. Unhelped by the uncritical support of family and isolated from the friends of the marriage whose embarrassment too often removes them entirely from the scene, there are few opportunities to resolve the conflicts. The very inability to come to any firm conclusions reduces self-confidence and self-esteem still further.

The Children

Most of the emotional responses to divorce are heightened by the presence of children. Feelings of guilt are exaggerated as one or both parents wonder whether further efforts should not have been made 'for the children's sake'. Feelings of inadequacy, already considerable, are increased: the very low emotional ebb that accompanies divorce is hardly the best condition in which to embark upon the hazards of single parent living.

The parent who is denied custody will often feel an acute sense of deprivation. Feelings of guilt may sometimes present this as a bitter but well-merited punishment. More often, it will be seen as unjust and unjustifiable and the scope for future complications will be endless. For some absent parents there will be the added frustration of being denied the opportunity to atone for the breakdown by attempting to make good the children's loss through the access relationship. For most, however, there is the disturbing knowledge that some continuing communion between them will be essential if access is to be made workable. For some of them at least there will be the even more disturbing knowledge that this can only be a source of further disharmony and ill feeling in the future.

The Unsevered Bond

Divorce is a purely legal remedy and as such it can only sever the legal aspects of the marriage bond. It is not responsible for the emotional ills which its processes both highlight and exacerbate and neither can it offer any cure for them. It is like a surgeon who, having performed the essential amputation of a mutilated and useless limb, is unable thereafter to treat the operational wound.

A couple know after the court hearing that they are divorced, at least on a provisional basis: there is documentary evidence to prove it. The final stage, the making of the decree absolute, occurs later without any formality at all. The petitioner applies to the court's administrative arm for the appropriate document which, if the necessary arrangements for the children's welfare have been declared satisfactory, is furnished automatically. At no stage has there been any attempt to bring home to the parties the emotional implications of divorce, for this is not the court's function. It is not, in any official sense, anyone's function. Yet intellectual acceptance alone is not sufficient to enable mourning for the lost relationship to proceed and far too many couples are left with an undischarged emotional commitment to it. Whether the commitment is mainly positive or mainly negative is unimportant. Its existence will not only hinder the development of the newly single personality, but will also make for a multitude of problems in any continuing relationship which may be necessary, as for example over the children.

One possible solution to this dilemma is offered by the growing practice in the United States of conducting ritual divorce ceremonies upon a specifically non-legal basis. Kathryn Hallett contrasts such a ritual with the hurtful experience of her own divorce which has been previously quoted (see pages 11–12):

> Years later when I watched Virginia Satir, a distinguished counsellor, perform a divorce ritual, my children and I cried our tears and relived our own situation. I envied that couple and their children, for they had a chance to participate in the letting go process. I watched the woman remove her ring and give back the obligations that he had given her. I listened to her tell what she would remember that was good and what she would forgive and forget. I looked at the children's faces as they watched their parents return their rings and promise to respect each other and continue to care for, support and love their children. The couple

> cried, their children cried and we all mourned the passing of an important event in their lives. We were there, too, when they rejoiced over their new freedom. The man told me that they'd been divorced for two years and were continually 'tearing each other up' until this day. They had refused to let go! Now he had shared his pain and joy with his whole family and could move on into another new relationship.[4]

Viewed with the reserve which is traditional upon this side of the Atlantic the ritual may appear at first sight to be flamboyant, over emotional and too typically American to have any relevance to our problems here. It is certainly true that we are probably too inhibited, apart from lacking the requisite skills, to incorporate any similar ceremony into our own divorce court welfare practice. The need which is identified is nonetheless a very real one. The absence of any formalized ritual of emotional divorce does not save people from the responses such a procedure evokes. If anything, it encourages these feelings to persist unrecognized, although they must in the end be experienced at a conscious level, like any other form of mourning, before the newly integrated personality can emerge. Nor should we be put off by the overtly emotional approach. Divorce does involve deeply felt emotions, and the inability to express them freely adds greatly to its hurt. It is at this level that the welfare officer must be prepared to get involved if he is to be able to offer any effective help in the conciliation process.

THE WELFARE OFFICER AS CONCILIATOR

What has emerged most clearly from this brief account of some of the social attitudes and personal responses to divorce is that many of its casualties do need the help of a counselling service which can complement the legal process of dissolution. The principal aims of this counselling are two fold: to achieve a level of conciliation that will enable the parties and their children to pursue their newly-based lives as complete and secure personalities, whilst conducting their post-marriage relationships with a maximum of harmony and good will; and to reduce as far as may be possible the damagingly divisive effects of whatever continuing legal proceedings may be necessary.

The task of conciliation is implicit in all that the welfare officer undertakes. The pursuit of it will often lead him into a much more broadly based involvement in the field of marriage breakdown than will his relatively circumscribed duties as a reporter to the court. The ordering of the report usually provides the initial entry to the situation and can often offer the stimulus to conciliation by its demand that attitudes and behaviour be examined and evaluated. The enquiry itself, however, may ultimately be overshadowed and outlived by the conciliation work which the parties themselves identify as the first priority. This is not in any way to devalue the reporting function which, besides acting as a trigger, has a critical importance of its own when conciliation fails. It is subsidiary in the sense only that its significance will necessarily diminish in direct proportion to the extent that conciliation is successful.

Conciliation in the Broken Marriage

Counselling with a view to conciliation after divorce is concerned with three main areas of difficulty. They are those that the individual experiences within himself in coming to terms with the fact of his divorce and its emotional repercussions upon him; those that stem specifically from attitudes towards and future relations with the former partner; and those that involve the relationships between divorced parents and their children. These perhaps somewhat arbitrary categories do of course overlap, with attitudes in any one influencing responses in either or both of the others. It is, however, important for the welfare officer to be able to identify them separately if his work is to have a sharp and appropriate focus. Without an accurate assessment of the principal area of difficulty he will be in danger of concentrating his attentions upon what may be only a secondary manifestation, which cannot successfully be manipulated in isolation.

Personal conciliation

This term is used to describe the work undertaken with the person who is so depressed and debilitated by divorce that he is not only unable to cope with the immediate demands of separate living, but is equally incapable of contemplating his single future as anything other than arid and meaningless. He is not necessarily beset with problems in relation to his former partner and his children. It is not so much, to borrow Kathryn Hallett's terminology, a case of not being able to let go; it is rather one of being left, after the event, with a self-image so shattered that there is no belief in the possibility of a satisfactory or satisfying life style in the single state.

The welfare officer's task is still one of conciliation, but it is one of conciliation with self rather than between the client and the members of his former family. Some elements of practical help may be involved initially, such as assisting in negotiations with other statutory bodies or providing introductions to appropriate social outlets, but the work will be based essentially upon the one to one relationship. The objective will be to build up self-esteem so that the client can begin to see himself again as a desirable and acceptable person, whilst facing up to the painful realities of what has indeed been lost. Some of the areas of self doubt which are identified may be the unreal products of his depression, whilst others will have a recognizable validity. The process of rebuilding the self-image will have to be based in reality, accepting and coming to terms with the limitations which are exposed as well as capitalizing upon the unrecognized strengths.

Conciliation between parents

Conciliation of this kind is called for when the problem is one of letting go. One of the parents may still wish, at least unconsciously, for a reconciliation, or one or both of them may need to go on fighting the unfinished marital battles. Emotional energies are being inappropriately focused as efforts are made to sustain a very personalized element in the post-divorce relationship. This will often give rise to problems over access as the children of the marriage become the victims of adult-orientated manoeuvres. This apparent determination to hark back to the past may be the symptom of a reluctance or an inability to face the prospect of a single future. Much insecurity and hurt will often lie behind the superficially aggressive facade in such cases.

The welfare officer's task here is to help the client to look forward rather than backwards. He may well lack the necessary self-confidence initially and the same process of rebuilding the self-image may be necessary as with the depressed and inward-looking client. He will also need to be released from the emotional tie which still binds him, and this will not be possible unless he is allowed to grieve for and to mourn the relationship which he is being asked to surrender. He will need help, therefore, in looking closely at his marriage, in its successful aspects as well as in those which precipitated its breakdown. He will need to understand why as well as where it fell short of expectations, for his partner as well as for himself. Greater understanding will help to reduce feelings of guilt for the breakdown on the one hand and of recrimination against the former partner on the other. In this relative emotional calm he may be able to gain some measure of insight, not only into the reasons for his present attitudes and behaviour, but also into the effect that they are having upon his former partner and his children. It is this last consideration, in particular, which may provide the motive for change.

Conciliation between parents and children

The proposition that divorce hurts children is accepted readily enough by most divorcing parents, and they will want to protect their children as far as they can. They are, however, frequently too caught up in their own distress to be able to appreciate the depth of their children's hurt or to recognize very readily the ways in which it is being expressed. This is an area of acute vulnerability for parents, whose own defensive mechanisms will often be at work in preventing too conscious an acknowledgement of their own part in producing their children's distress. The responsibility may be displaced onto adolescence, or school – where problems may be symptoms of that distress – or, most commonly, onto the deliberate machinations of the other parent. It is difficult in the extreme for parents to accept that they may themselves have contributed, although perhaps unavoidably, to the awkward, anti-social or openly rejecting behaviour of their children, and it is an area which calls for the most sensitive of counselling.

Children will often need personal counselling in the face of their confused and angry responses to their parents' divorce. Many of them will harbour quite inappropriate feelings of guilt for the event and when these are heightened by additional feelings of ambivalence and perhaps of open hostility, the burden can become well nigh intolerable. Such feelings need to be expressed, accepted and understood. It may be necessary to explore with them ideas about parents still loving though leaving, and about children still being allowed to love. Conflicting loyalties must be accepted as painful as well as natural; the seemingly easy option of rejecting one parent totally may need to be examined for its shortcomings as well as for its offer of immediate ease.

There will be occasions when there is no easy solution. The child's reasons for rejecting his parent may be compelling and a continuing estrangement may be the only answer. The task of conciliation with both parent and child will then be a very real one, as the fact of separation has to be accepted as well as understood. Rarely will total separation be seen as permanently desirable. The channels for future communication must be kept open as attitudes and feelings are further explored and perhaps modified. Conciliation here involves very much the avoidance of extreme stances, containing the desire for a frontal assault on the problem on the one hand and working against the possibility of a final and total rejection on the other. Reconciliation may never be attainable in some cases but the final hurt of an unreasoning and uncomprehending rejection may at least be prevented.

Conciliation and the Legal Process

Besides attempting to mitigate the effects of divorce upon the parties and their children at an individual level and seeking for agreed solutions to their continuing differences, the welfare officer in his role as conciliator has a function to fulfil in relation to the legal proceedings themselves. This must be so because, although the mechanics of dissolution have moved as far as is practicable in the direction of reducing the elements of public trauma and humiliation, it is in the nature of divorce and its ancillary proceedings that it should be divisive in its effect. It has, as it were, been tacitly acknowledged that the point of possible compromise has been passed and confrontation is accepted by those involved as the order of the day. The parties have already been distanced by the decision to take the matter to court. The fact that material of a highly personal nature has to be committed to paper to be seen by total strangers adds to the effect. Petitions and affidavits do not pretend to present other than a one-sided view and even when individual episodes are faithfully recorded, they can appear as a damaging betrayal when presented outside the context of the marriage as a whole.

To this must be added the greatest single handicap of our legal system, which bedevils all domestic proceedings. This is that they are conducted upon an adversarial rather than an inquisitorial basis. That is to say that the parties are in open opposition to each other, with each trying to establish the merits of his own case and destroy the substance of his opponent's, rather than attempting directly to establish where the true facts of the situation lie. This is particularly important in disputes over custody and access. The court may be charged with the duty of safeguarding the interests of the child, but the parties will too often see the matter exclusively in terms of winning or losing. Too little, sadly, is done by many of their legal advisors to alter their perceptions. Disputes over children, handled in this way, can degenerate too easily into attacks upon the character, competence and veracity of the opposing party. This rarely helps to resolve the issue in the child's interests and the damage which it can do to the future relationship between the parents is incalculable.

It is in this arena of bitter confrontation, which the whole ethos of our legal system tends to perpetuate rather than to diminish, that the welfare officer must seek to conciliate. It is not an easy task. Many parents are able to convince themselves that what they want so passionately for their children would also be in their best interests, and nothing in the legal process to date is likely to have dissuaded them from the view that it is not only their right but almost their duty to fight for it to the last ditch. Many fundamental assumptions will have to be re-examined before they are able even to consider the possibility that it could be desirable for the child's sake to abandon or to cease to oppose any given application. Conciliation is thus not only related to the specific dispute before the court, but is extended to cover all the feelings of hostility and all the predetermined and rigid stances which the institution of legal proceedings is usually taken to imply.

It should not be assumed because of the stress which has been placed upon it that conciliation constitutes any kind of universal panacea. Parents will continue to disagree profoundly about where the best interests of their children lie, and it is and should be their right to test their views before the court. Conciliation techniques can not be pressed beyond the point at which parties offer their willing cooperation, for otherwise they would be denied their right of hearing and in effect fall victim to an unofficial or extra-legal adjudication. It is not to be expected that conciliation will always provide specific answers to contested issues: the nature of the disputes is such that it will indeed fail to do so more often than it succeeds. But the finding of specific solutions is not the whole task and perhaps not always the most important part of it. What it will always attempt, albeit again with varying degrees of success, is to help parents to clarify the issues that are really in dispute, and test whether they are truly pursuing the welfare of the child or whether some other still unresolved problem is obtruding. Where the well-being of the child is the genuine matter in contention, it can perhaps serve to reduce some of the bitterness engendered, and prevent the conducting of a hate-filled campaign against the former partner.

THE WELFARE OFFICER AS REPORTER

It is in his role as reporter, when the court orders a welfare enquiry, that the welfare officer will usually first meet the family with whom he works. His formal task will be to provide the court with both factual information and professional assessment and opinion when issues involving children are to be determined. A detailed account of the different types of report which are prepared and the method and extent of the enquiries involved is provided in Chapter 5. The more general purpose at this stage is to highlight some of the characteristics of the reporting as opposed to the conciliating role, and to contrast it with that of the probation officer reporting in criminal proceedings.

The Comparison of Intangibles

The welfare officer has been described as the eyes and ears of the divorce court judge, an observation which conveys something of the range of enquiry that is expected of him and the type of comment that may form a legitimate part of his report. Factual information must be provided and it will indeed be of critical importance on occasion. More commonly, however, it will be no more than the skeleton upon which is built those assessments of the less tangible features of the case that are at the heart of the report.

Material considerations will often play no significant part in access applications, particularly when the contact proposed is a limited one. Even in questions of custody and of staying access they will be important only to the extent of establishing that proper physical care is available. Few cases are determined upon such issues. The matter is much more likely to hinge upon the personalities and attitudes of the parents and upon the likelihood or otherwise of the child thriving in an emotional sense in a given environment. Assessment at this more complex level, and not only assessment but valid comparison, is likely to offer more real assistance to the court than any amount of factual information about the parties and their material circumstances.

It is in this area of comparison of intangible factors, and of assessing the likely consequences for the child of the disposals available to the court, that the interaction with the conciliation role becomes crucial. The attitudes that parents display towards their former marriages and former partners can influence profoundly their performances as custodial parents and in the access situation. These are less likely to emerge in the course of straightforward enquiry than in the more positively helpful context of attempted conciliation. It is here that both they and the welfare officer are most likely to find some understanding of the patterns of behaviour which are manifested; the alternative of description without explanation is of comparatively little help to the court or to the parties. This does imply a very clear exposition of the welfare officer's dual role at the outset, but provided that the parties are aware that all the material which emerges may be used at the reporting stage, the possibility of problems of confidentiality can be reduced to a minimum.

Secondary Sources of Information

The welfare officer is not bound in his report by the formal rules of evidence. That is to say that he does not have to restrict himself to such information as he is able formally to verify at first hand. He is allowed wide discretion and he can contact any one who he thinks may assist in his enquiries; he will normally be expected to consult with teachers, doctors and other agencies who may have relevant knowledge of the family. He is permitted, subject to suitable consents being obtained, to quote both information and opinion derived from such sources. He is also permitted to comment himself upon this information and opinion, and to indicate whether it conflicts or is in accord with his own findings and with the overall picture which is being built up.[5]

Secondary sources of information of this kind tend to play a more significant part in divorce enquiries than in other reports to the court. This is partly because the welfare report is the product of a much more comprehensive pattern of enquiry, conducted over a comparatively lengthy period of time. There is perhaps also a greater need to present the parties in their total life situations; the relatively narrow focus of the social enquiry report is not appropriate to the determination of matters relating to the children's welfare, to which so much more is relevant and which in consequence demands presentation upon the broadest possible canvas.

Since part of his task is to gather together and to synthesize all the relevant information, the welfare officer cannot work in isolation. This does not mean, however, that he can share his ultimate responsibility; the selection of suitable avenues for exploration and the balancing and interpretation of the information he obtains falls to him alone. Realistic evaluation will rarely be possible unless the newly-acquired information is shared with the parties to whom it relates. If this process helps them better to understand their situation and their responses to it, the role of conciliator will again be seen to be impinging upon the reporting function.

The Child as Client

The ordering of a welfare officer's report, other than in pre-decree and satisfaction cases where the central issue of the child's welfare is readily apparent, will usually stem from the court's need for assistance in resolving a parental dispute over a child. The attitude which the welfare officer adopts in relation to the parental conflict must be one of strict neutrality: he must not be seen to be championing the cause of one parent against the other. He will, of course, be required to assess the merits of the parents' conflicting claims, but only in the course of attempting to establish where the child's best interests lie. If he should reach a conclusion which supports the application of one parent rather than the other, this will not invalidate the essential impartiality of his position. The fact that his assessment of the child's best interests happens to coincide with the wishes of that particular parent is in a sense incidental: the criterion of the child's welfare may equally lead to a conclusion which finds favour with neither of them.

This is in marked contrast to the conciliator's role, in which either parent may be the principal client, or they may share that status equally. At the reporting stage the child must occupy the central position, because it is his welfare which is paramount. This need not be reflected in purely quantitative terms in the written report. It will often be appropriate to devote far more space to the personalities and attitudes of the parents than to those of the child himself. He will nonetheless remain the principal focus of the report. The parents do not figure in it as he does, in their own right, but only insofar as their wishes in respect of him are concerned, and their abilities to translate them into an emotionally healthy pattern of child care.

Status of the Welfare Report

The welfare report in custody and access issues enjoys an appreciably higher status than the social enquiry report in criminal proceedings. This does not derive simply from the fact that it is a much more detailed and comprehensive document and is based upon a much longer and more exhaustive process of investigation. The reason is that the welfare report is always central to the court's deliberations in a way that the social enquiry report can rarely be. In a criminal case, and especially where serious offences are involved, the judge must be mindful of many issues simultaneously. Sentencing policy, public safety, the possible deterrent value of the sentence imposed and the previous record of the defendant may all influence his thinking: the welfare of the offender upon whom the report has been prepared may occupy a relatively lowly position in the priorities which he has to balance. In a custody or access case on the other hand, the court has a single and overriding priority, the welfare of the child, and it is to this specific end that the welfare officer's report has been prepared. It is the only document before the court which is directed exclusively and impartially to the one all-important issue and it is from this that its significance and its status are derived.

Judicial Attitudes

The enhanced status of welfare reports over the past decade is also a result of a developing judicial awareness of the need for detailed information and informed professional comment upon the issues to be determined. This is typified by the now almost universal practice of ordering welfare reports in all contested issues. Most judges do now accord considerable weight to the views expressed by their welfare officers, and it has indeed been suggested, in Clark v Clark (1970), that the court should state its reasons when it reaches a different conclusion. This is in most respects a desirable situation from the welfare point of view, but it is important that the judge should be and be seen to be the final arbiter. The welfare officer must always remember that his recommendations are no more than suggestions to the court and that the field of judicial decision is not his to tread.

The clear distinction between enquiry and recommendation on the one hand and legal adjudication on the other should be scrupulously maintained. A judge who is too dependent upon the recommendations of his welfare officer can too easily cast him in the combined role of judge, jury and executioner. This is fair neither to the welfare officer nor his client and it can indeed have disastrous repercussions upon their future working relationship. The welfare officer should be seen only to have offered his considered professional opinion to the court; even when his proposals are adopted in their entirety, the final decision must be recognized as the court's and the court's alone.

3

Custody

The legal custody of legitimate children was traditionally held at common law to be vested in the father. It was only with the passing of the Guardianship Act of 1973 that mothers were accorded equality of parental rights. This equality still obtains after separation or divorce, with both parents remaining the joint custodians of their children unless and until the court makes an order to the contrary.

THE LEGAL BACKGROUND

Section 42(1) of the Matrimonial Causes Act 1973 empowers the court to:

> make such order as it thinks fit for the custody and education of any child of the family who is under the age of eighteen –
>
> (a) in any proceedings for divorce, nullity of marriage or judicial separation, before or on granting a decree or at any time thereafter (whether, in the case of a decree of divorce or nullity of marriage, before or after the decree is made absolute);
>
> (b) where any such proceedings are dismissed after the beginning of the trial, either forthwith or within a reasonable period after the dismissal.
>
> and . . . it may instead, if it thinks fit, direct that proper proceedings be taken for making the child a ward of court.

A child of the family is defined under Section 52(1) of the Act as

> (a) a child of both the parties, and
>
> (b) any other child, not being a child who has been boarded out

> with those parties by a local authority or voluntary organisation, who has been treated by both of those parties as a child of their family.[1]

The power of the court to vary its orders for custody is to be found under Section 42(7) of the Act, which states:

> The court shall have the power to vary or discharge an order made under this section or to suspend any provision thereof temporarily and to revive the operation of any provision so suspended.

The authority of the court in matters of custody is thus very extensive indeed. Orders can be made at any time from the filing of the petition until the child of the family reaches the age of 18; they can contain any provision which the court thinks fit to include; they can be varied, suspended or restored at need; and they can apply equally, without any precisely defined time limit, in those cases where the substantive proceedings are dismissed. In short, it is fair to say that once the court is seized of the issue, it retains the power to make whatever further orders may be necessary in the child's interest, until he passes by virtue of his age beyond its jurisdiction.

Custody and Care and Contol

The court may on occasion make an order which separates the element of care and control from full legal custody and it is therefore necessary to distinguish between these two concepts.

Custody

The concept of custody embraces all the duties which a parent owes to his child. These include feeding and clothing him and providing him with an adequate home; providing him with protection, discipline and control; ensuring that he receives a proper education, and determining the nature of his religious upbringing.

Custody in modern times is concerned more or less exclusively with the obligations which parenthood imposes. It used to include as well the services that a parent could properly expect from his child. Happily this aspect is now almost totally disregarded.

Care and control

The term 'care and control' is used to describe those aspects of custody which are concerned with the day to day management of the child. It will thus include feeding, clothing and housing him and providing him with an environment conducive to his proper physical and emotional development. It will not include the taking of major decisions which affect his long term future in such matters as education and religious upbringing. The management of his financial assets and the giving of consent to his marriage will similarly be excluded.

The Orders Available to the Court

The fact that the court may make a distinction between custody on the one hand and care and control on the other opens up a variety of possibilities as to the final form of the order. Custody, care and control may be given to one parent; custody to one and care and control to the other; or custody jointly to both parents with care and control to one of them. There is also provision to grant custody or care and control to a third party, again with or without the two being similarly divided. In appropriate cases the child may, as an alternative, be committed to the care of the local authority. A parent may, in exceptional circumstances, be declared unfit to have custody. A supervision order may be made in conjunction with any of these orders, other than a care order, should the court consider this to be necessary. The criteria for the making of supervision orders and questions relating to their management are considered in Chapter 6.

Custody

A simple and unqualified order for custody gives custody, care and control to one parent, investing in him all the rights and duties which were formerly held jointly by both. The order will normally include a provision which allows access to the absent parent. This is much the most common type of order, meeting as it does the needs of the majority of cases.

The split order

The split order grants custody to one parent and care and control to the other. The circumstances in which it is appropriate are implicit in the boundaries of the care and control concept: in essence, the court must be satisfied that although one parent is the better suited to have charge of the child on a day to day basis, there are circumstances which make it undesirable for that parent to be given exclusive responsibility for his upbringing. A typical case would be one in which the court is loath to deprive a child of his mother's immediate care, but entertains some reservations nonetheless as to her ability to cater for all his needs on a long term basis. Substantial differences between the parents in matters of education or religious upbringing may also contribute to a decision in favour of a split order. Less appropriately perhaps, split orders are sometimes made when the court is reluctant to exclude a 'deserving' father from the major decisions which affect his child's future.

From a welfare point of view, split orders seem often to create as many problems as they solve. Parents are frequently confused about the division of their duties and responsibilities. An order for custody is too often misinterpreted as a licence to interfere in the daily management of the child, whilst the parent with care and control only may feel inhibited and threatened as well as devalued by the limitations imposed upon him. Difficulties over access are also common; many custodial parents fail to appreciate that they have no greater rights in determining how and when and where access shall take place than any other parents who are not responsible for the daily care of their children.

It is relatively unusual for parents to seek or to be happy with a split order. There are few who are so well adjusted after divorce that they are able to consult harmoniously about their children's future, when the consultation is legally forced upon them in this fashion. Whilst the order may be desirable in theory, the problems of making it work in practice can be formidable; they can indeed give rise to greater difficulties than those which it was originally designed to overcome. Unless the evidence in support of a split order is overwhelming, the welfare officer should be extremely cautious about recommending it.

Joint custody

As an alternative to the split order, the court may grant the custody of a child jointly to both parents whilst giving care and control to one of them. The indications for joint custody are broadly the same as for a split order, except that the intention is to allow both parents to retain an equal voice in questions affecting the child's future.

Joint custody is sometimes sought by parents who are properly anxious that each of them should be seen to be playing as full and active a part as possible in the upbringing of their children. Many judges are content to make such orders if both parents are in favour; some, indeed, impose them on occasion regardless of parental wishes. They should be approached with caution, even when parents are pressing in their requests, for they suffer from the same pitfalls as split orders. However good their initial intentions, parents may find themselves in disagreement about their children's future; circumstances can change radically, and attitudes with them. Not only will ill feeling and disharmony then result but possibly situations of total deadlock as well, since neither parent can make a decision that prevails.

The joint custody order appears to have little merit, beyond a somewhat specious acknowledgement of the absent parent's continued involvement with his child. If parents are minded to consult with each other over their children they will do so, whether or not any formal obligation is laid upon them. If they are not, the existence of the order will not make them any more likely to reach agreement. A cynic might be forgiven for concluding that when the order works it is unnecessary and when it is necessary it is unworkable.

Custody to a third party

It is possible for a person other than one of the divorcing parents to apply to the court for leave to intervene in the divorce proceedings and then to apply, with the official status of an intervenor, for the custody of a child of the family. This procedure is usually adopted by grandparents or other relatives who already have *de facto* custody of the child and wish to ensure that this arrangement is not disturbed as a result of the divorce. The intervenor may also apply for or be granted care and control only, with custody remaining with one or both of the parents. An alternative procedure is for the relatives to institute wardship proceedings instead of seeking leave to intervene in the divorce action. If the wardship application succeeds custody remains with the court, but care and control may be granted to the applicants if this is considered to be in the child's interests.

If the intervenor's application is not opposed by either of the parents, the court may as a precaution order a welfare report – the enquiry will be akin to one for satisfaction – before making the proposed consent order. If it is opposed the court will almost certainly require a full welfare enquiry, in which case the proposals and the circumstances of the intervenor will be investigated and reported upon in the same way as those of the contesting parents.

Declaration of unfitness

The court has the power under Section 42(3) of the Act to include in a decree of divorce or judicial separation: 'a declaration that either party in the marriage in question is unfit to have the custody of the children of the family'. The effect of such a declaration, as described in Section 42(4), is that

> if the party to whom the declaration relates is a parent of any child of the family, that party shall not, on the death of the other parent, be entitled as of right to the custody or guardianship of that child.

This is clearly an extreme remedy and it is employed only in extreme circumstances. It is designed to protect children against the danger of falling by default into the charge of a parent who is manifestly unfitted to care for them. This might apply to a parent suffering from serious mental illness or impairment, or to one with convictions for grave offences of a sexual or violent nature.

Care order

Section 42(1) of the Act empowers the court to make an order committing the care of a child to the local authority if: 'it appears to the court that there are exceptional circumstances making it impracticable or undesirable for the child to be entrusted to either of the parties to the marriage or to any other individual'.

The wording of this section makes it clear that committal to care is seen as a last resort, appropriate only when neither parent nor any third party is considered a suitable custodian. It is essentially a discretionary matter, an order which the court may make 'if it thinks fit'. There is no formal test to be applied, as in care proceedings before a juvenile court. It does not have to be proved that the child is being neglected, ill-treated or exposed to moral danger, or whatever the substance of the complaint may be; and neither need it be proved that he is in need of care and control which he would be unlikely to receive unless an order were made. 'Exceptional circumstances making it impracticable or undesirable' is a much looser and more subjective test. Technically at least, it is possible for a child to be committed to care in divorce proceedings in circumstances which would fail to meet the more rigorous requirements of the juvenile court process.

Custody as a Legal Remedy

It has already been suggested that the adversarial basis of our legal system makes it relatively unsuitable for the resolving of domestic disputes and that this applies particularly in cases where children are involved. Attitudes tend to become polarized as a result of it and there is some danger of parents pursuing their individual vendettas rather than seeking only to secure the best interests of their children. It would be too much to suggest that the child's welfare is actually disregarded, but there are tempting opportunities in the course of proceedings which ostensibly relate to him alone, to resurrect old quarrels and perhaps settle some old scores in passing.

Despite this obvious limitation, issues of disputed custody are at least more amenable to formal legal adjudication than are those of disputed access. In the vast majority of cases the court will be deciding between the directly conflicting claims of the child's parents. The decision may well be extremely difficult, but it is still one of straightforward choice in what amounts to an either/or situation. There will be few occasions upon which the actual custody decision will need to be qualified to any appreciable extent.

Hurtful and distressing though recourse to legal adjudication may be, some parents at least may welcome it in some respects. The problem has already proved insoluble to them and the possibility of a clear-cut decision for which they themselves do not have to bear the final responsibility is not without its attractions.

THE WELFARE PRINCIPLE

The governing principle for judges in the determination of custody issues is set down in Section 1 of the Guardianship of Minors Act 1971. This section, which re-enacts the first section of the Guardianship of Infants Act 1925 states that:

> where in any proceedings before any court . . . the custody or upbringing of a minor . . . is in question, the court, in deciding that question, shall regard the welfare of the minor as the first and paramount consideration.

Although the Guardianship of Minors Act obviously preceded the Matrimonial Causes Act 1973 which embodies the bulk of current divorce legislation, the principle identified in it still holds good. The phrase 'in any proceedings before any court' applies to subsequent as well as previous enactments which are concerned with the custody of children. The authoritative interpretation of the phrase 'first and paramount' is to be found in Lord MacDermott's speech in the House of Lords in the case of J v C (1969). The relevant passage runs:

> . . . when all the relevant facts, relationships, claims and wishes of the parents, risks, choices and other circumstances are taken into account and weighed, the course to be followed will be that which is most in the interests of the child's welfare as that term had now to be understood. That is the first consideration because it is of first importance and the paramount consideration because it rules or determines the course to be followed.

To this may be added the Court of Appeal judgment in S(BD) v S(DJ) of 1977 in which it was stated that: 'The question is not what the essential justice of the case requires but what the best interest of the children requires.' This judgment, also confirmed in Re K (minors) in the same year, was also important in that it removed what had hitherto been held to be a qualification of the welfare principle in the guise of the so-called unimpeachable parent. It established decisively that the wishes of a parent, however blameless in the context of the marriage breakdown, cannot take precedence over the best interests of the child.

This must be guidance enough for the practising welfare officer in reaching his conclusions. He may consider it anomalous that no statute declares the welfare of the child to be the single and absolute consideration, but he will still be well advised to treat it as such in any recommendation he may make to the court.

GUIDELINES FOR CUSTODY DECISIONS

Although the welfare principle is of fundamental importance it is presented in terms which are much too general to offer any specific guidelines as to how individual contested custody issues should be determined. There is no attempt to define what constitutes the welfare of a child and no formal categorization of the various factors which should be taken into account in reaching a decision. Considerable importance must therefore attach to the question of precedent, of how judges have interpreted the concept of welfare in the past and what they have seen as the critical issues in determining disputes over custody.

Precedents must nonetheless be treated with some caution. Ideas as to how best a child's interests may be safeguarded will vary from time to time according to the prevailing social and moral climate. Attitudes which were accepted as proper and appropriate in their time may later be considered to have but little relevance. Adulterous mothers were in the past effectively debarred from custody, while the fathers of young or girl children were denied any real opportunity to care for them as single parents. These stances have been modified very substantially as society's perceptions of such mothers and such fathers have become more realistic and more enlightened.

There are not, or should not be any rigid and absolute standards, since interpretations of what constitutes good child care and of children's emotional needs are not static. The broad guide lines which prevail at the present time should not therefore be seen as being representative of anything more than the current consensus of opinion. It must be remembered too that every case must be judged upon its individual merits: there may always be a sufficient reason for reaching a conclusion which runs contrary to the existing pattern.

Subject to these reservations it is still helpful to examine some of the main guidelines which are currently in force, and to consider their implications in terms of today's social work thinking and practice.

Preservation of the Status Quo

Possession is proverbially nine points of the law and nowhere is this more apparent than in the contested custody issue. Other than in the relatively rare emergency application, the matter will not come before the court until quite an appreciable time after the parental separation. The children will by then have had some opportunity to come to terms with the loss of one of their parents and to adjust to living with the remaining one. A reversal of the existing arrangement would demand considerable fresh adjustments, could well induce renewed feelings of insecurity and would inevitably be traumatic to a degree. The proposed alternative, moreover, however desirable in theory, will rarely have been tested in practice, except perhaps in the highly artificial context of staying access. Given that the children have made a reasonable initial adjustment and that the parent with whom they are living is providing a satisfactory standard of care, it is scarcely surprising that the courts should be reluctant to interfere. The risks involved, for what must always to some extent be a questionable return, may simply appear too great.

The case for preserving the *status quo* presupposes some measure of acceptance of the existing custody arrangement on the part of the children. In practice this proves to be the case more often than not, because their need for security following the loss of one parent will generally be acute enough to inhibit any open conflict with the one who has remained. Some obviously will accept it more readily than others, with responses ranging from positive contentment on the one hand to passive toleration on the other. But whatever the level of acceptance, it will carry with it a complementary implication of rejection of the absent parent. This rejection, especially in the early stages after separation, will often be the children's only defence against an otherwise intolerable conflict of loyalties. The more positively they align themselves with the existing arrangement, the more pronounced the rejection will appear to be. An extreme response may also be a form of opting out, an unconscious recognition of the equally powerful but opposing emotions to which they cannot afford to give expression. Most children will need time and some of them professional counselling before they feel able to love and be loved by the departed one. Unless the case for a change of custody is compelling, there is good reason not to enforce it before these highly ambivalent feelings have been worked through and some genuine stability of emotions achieved.

The case against maintaining the *status quo* can of course be powerful as well, either on an initial application or upon a later attempt to vary an established arrangement. Sheer force of circumstances may result in children being left with the obviously less suitable partner when parents separate. Where this is not the case, situations and attitudes can alter sufficiently for initially sound arrangements to fail to meet their needs at a later stage. Parents may take new partners, or separate from them; they may cope better or less well than anticipated with the aftermath of divorce; children themselves can undergo profound changes of attitude as they mature and their perceptions sharpen. Life moves forward for all, for the betterment of some and to the disadvantage of others, and this is bound to be reflected at times in the reversal as well as in the confirmation of existing custody arrangements. The fact remains in practice that the benefit of the doubt, if one may borrow a sporting analogy, is usually given to the defending side. This is surely as it should be; it is the applicant parent who is seeking to alter the existing arrangement and it is upon him that the onus of demonstrating that this would be in his child's best interests very properly falls.

The case of Rachel is a good example of the preservation of the *status quo* as the determining factor in a finely balanced custody issue. Rachel was an only child who had remained with her father when mother left the matrimonial home; she was then six years old. Significantly, she had not seen her mother for several months thereafter. Mother remarried as soon as the divorce became absolute and moved to a different part of the country. Staying access was introduced on an informally agreed basis and despite occasional difficulties it proved a positive experience; Rachel established a satisfactory relationship with her mother's husband, who took a genuine interest in her.

Mother enjoyed the better material circumstances and was able and anxious to provide exceptionally generously for her daughter. The former matrimonial home, on the other hand, in which father and Rachel still lived, was quite adequate and it had the added advantage of being the one which the child had known from birth. Rachel was well cared for there by the housekeeper whom father had employed for that purpose and with whom she enjoyed a warm and affectionate relationship.

Although Rachel had been much distressed at the time of her parents' separation, she had achieved some measure of equilibrium when the custody issue was finally heard some 12 months later. She was reported by the welfare officer to be at ease in both her parents' homes and to have indicated no firm preference to live with one of them rather than the other. The welfare officer was influenced to some extent by the more relaxed personality of the father as compared with that of his somewhat neurotic former wife. A more telling factor was that the child had, by reason of daily proximity, developed a relationship of proven worth with her mother-substitute at home which had no parallel in her occasional access relationship with her mother's husband. Both these factors were, however, only subsidiary to the main conclusion they supported, which was that Rachel's most pressing need was for the continuity, stability and security which could only be provided in the environment she had always known. This view was endorsed by the court and despite the mother's obviously powerful claim to bring up her small daughter in circumstances which would have bordered on the opulent, custody remained with the father.

The Presumption in the Mother's Favour

Although the time has long passed since a father's only effective chance of obtaining the custody of his children rested upon the sexual misconduct of his wife, it is probably true to say that there is still some continuing element of prejudice in favour of the mother. The removal of the bar against the adulterous wife retaining custody, although most proper and desirable in itself, has further weighted the balance in the same direction. The strong support for the view that small children need a full time parent, again unexceptionable in itself, tends in practice to support the mother's claim, which is further enhanced by the widely held opinion that all young children, and especially girl children, are better in her charge. The emergence in recent years of pressure groups such as 'Families Need Fathers' leaves no room for doubt that many fathers do still see themselves as being seriously disadvantaged in contested custody cases.

Parental roles have become much more readily interchangeable over the past 20 years and it is generally acknowledged that an increasing number of fathers are competent in most aspects of child care, even with very young children. This is reflected up to a point in custody decisions. The greater recognition which is given to the importance of continuity and stability in upbringing can, as was seen in Rachel's case, serve on occasion to defeat even well-founded maternal applications. On the whole, however, judicial thinking in this area has tended to lag a little behind social change. The lingering reluctance to confirm fathers such as Rachel's in the custody of their children is very much less evident when the parental situations are reversed.

From a social work point of view the stress should be laid upon treating every case on its individual merits. The presumption in the mother's favour then becomes less strong. The bond between a young child and his mother-figure is still seen to be of central importance, but the maternal relationship as such is perhaps considered less sacrosanct than it once was. There is more emphasis on the quality of mothering which is available and rather less insistence upon the fact that it should be the natural mother who provides it. This does often offer greater possibilities to the capable and caring father, especially when he has the support of a suitable surrogate mother. His case is further strengthened when, as with Rachel, it is the mother who leaves the home and breaks the continuity of the care. The assumption of many mothers that they can leave their children until it is convenient to resume caring for them, confident that the court will not hesitate to restore them to their charge, is proving ill-founded in an increasing number of cases.

Separation of Children

Legal convention and good social work practice are at one in holding that brothers and sisters should not be separated as a result of a custody decision other than in the most exceptional of circumstances. The suggestion that children should be divided up between their parents after divorce is in practice a relatively unusual one. Even the most embattled of parents can usually see far enough to realize that custody should generally be an all or nothing decision, with the children at least left with the immediate solace of each other's company and the subsequent advantage of growing up together. On the rare occasions when parents are prepared to barter on a crude 'one for you, one for me' basis, their insights into their children's needs should be considered suspect and their caring capabilities on the emotional plane most carefully examined.

Exceptions may occur occasionally, most often in the case of older children, who may perhaps already have begun to grow apart in their interests and outlook. Teenage children, who are effectively of an age to make their own decisions and who may not always identify with the same parent, can sometimes challenge the general principle very strongly.

> Brian and Jennifer, aged 16 and 13, were two such children. Their parents, although awaiting the hearing of a contested divorce cause, with adultery alleged by father and unreasonable behaviour by mother, were still living under the same roof. Each parent had much to complain of in the conduct of the other and no attempt was made to conceal their bitter mutual hatred. The house had for months been divided between them and lengthy periods of acute though uncommunicated tension were punctuated by episodes of quite serious physical violence.
>
> Both parents were seeking interim custody of both children. Father alleged that his wife was condoning and indeed encouraging promiscuity on Jennifer's part. Mother contended that her

husband encouraged Brian to be abusive and violent towards her. The welfare officer considered that each parent's interest was limited to the child of his or her own sex. The cross applications for custody of both children and the counter-allegations of bad parenting were in his view concerned more with establishing their claims to the sole tenancy of their jointly allocated council house than with any real regard for the children's welfare.

Jennifer had identified very strongly with her mother's cause from the outset, as Brian had done with his father's, and each had taken up residence in the home accordingly. Jennifer ate, cooked and slept with mother and Brian with father; attending different schools, they scarcely saw one another at all. Both children made serious allegations against the opposing parent, ranging from physical assault to attempts to secure perjured evidence, and each was adamant in refusing to consider any alteration in the *de facto* custody arrangements. Whilst each expressed the wish to maintain contact with the other, this consideration was far outweighed by the desire to escape permanently from the hostile parent; any suggestion of access was rejected out of hand.

Intervention by the welfare officer at the behest of the court resulted in each parent being offered a new council tenancy, and interim custody orders were made in accordance with the children's wishes. An order for mutual reasonable access, designed to allow the children to see each other, proved wholly unworkable and they and their respective parents went their entirely separate ways.

To attempt to compel a wholly unwilling compliance from one of these children solely in order to abide by a fixed principle would have been manifestly wrong; they had in fact already taken the only practicable decision for themselves. Exceptions such as this will occur occasionally to test the rule and the welfare principle may, as here, demand that it be broken. Happily, however, such extreme exceptions tend to be very few and far between.

Conduct in the Marriage

The conduct of the parties within a marriage is not held to be relevant to the issue of custody unless the conduct complained of is such as to cast doubt upon that parent's ability to provide the child with a proper upbringing. It is accepted that to be a 'bad' husband or wife is not necessarily the same thing as to be a 'bad' parent.

It is true that some of the factors which go to make a person an unsatisfactory husband or wife may also be such as to cast doubt upon his or her suitability as a parent. The mentally unstable, the alcoholic, the sexually deviant and the uncontrollably violent offer obvious examples. The line is less easy to draw in other cases. Sexual promiscuity, for example, can present the problem of balancing a warm, loving and caring attitude towards children against an unsuitable moral climate and the dangers of a succession of transient substitute parent figures. In other cases, behaviour which may be totally unacceptable within the context of a particular marriage may not reflect adversely upon a person's capabilities as a parent.

This was true of Sandra. An intelligent and physically attractive girl, without formal education and from a relatively humble background, she had married very young a man ten years her senior, with whom she had almost nothing in common. A rising member of the medical profession from an upper-middle class family, he was conservative, humourless and possessed of an air of no little rectitude. His parents made no secret of the fact that they believed him to have married unwisely and no attempt was made to welcome Sandra into the closely knit extended family. Her natural exuberance and spontaneity were efficiently stifled and the birth of her two sons in the first four years of marriage made her feel all the more trapped in an alien environment. After they started school she began to dissociate herself more and more emphatically from her husband's standards and from his family. Her friendships, on the fringes of the pop music scene, were strongly disapproved of and her adoption of its fashions of speech and dress completed the alienation. A brief affair was the occasion for divorce and her prayer for custody of the boys was hotly contested. She was presented in all too facile a manner as both irresponsible and immoral, and despite her very real affectionate and caring qualities as a mother, custody was denied her.

Her husband, in the event, had neither the time nor the inclination to care personally for his sons, who were left more and more in the care of his ailing mother. Sandra's contention that he was concerned only to impose his own rigid ideas on child-rearing, whilst punishing her for rejecting the standards he had been brought up by, seemed uncomfortably close to the truth. She sought over the next four years both to demonstrate that she was a responsible and capable parent – though without making any concessions to the much more relaxed and casual life style which she had now adopted completely – and to obtain a reversal of the original custody order.

Neither boy was happy in the structured and claustrophobic style of living in the grandparents' home and matters came to a head when they refused to leave their mother after a weekend's access. Here Sandra determined to make her stand, even in the face of an application to commit her to prison for contempt. A discerning judge insisted upon a full enquiry before taking any action and decided finally to grant her custody. A supervision order provided further monitoring and in an unusually happy outcome she not only proved herself to be a very capable and responsible mother, but achieved in the process a lasting measure of conciliation with her husband and his parents.

Cultural Factors

The growth of immigrant communities in post-war Britain has given rise to a new and sensitive set of problems in the determination of custody issues. This obtains equally whether the broken marriage is a mixed one or whether the parents are of the same ethnic origin. The broad principle adopted is that no child should be deprived of contact with his country of origin or with the culture in which he has been raised as a result of a custody decision. Whilst the principle is clearly sound, its application can nonetheless be problematic.

Much of the difficulty, for court and welfare officer alike, lies in an incomplete understanding of the cultural expectations of the parties in both marriage and divorce. Many immigrants are equally uncertain of or confused by the expectations of our society. In a mixed marriage the perceptions of the parties may be significantly at variance with each other, whilst either party to a wholly immigrant marriage may have grafted on to his or her own cultural expectations such aspects of western practice as appear to suit the immediate purpose. Insofar as any exposure to the English system of family law is likely to raise important issues of both principle and practice, some areas of confusion and doubt seem virtually inevitable.

Cultures such as those of the Indian sub-continent in which male authority and predominance automatically embraces the question of custody can present formidable problems. So far as the men are concerned, the welfare principle may appear totally irrelevant. Whether the wives who oppose them are Europeans who have been brought up to see the mother's role as crucially important, or Asians who are brought to a realization of their relatively favoured position before an English court, the loss of face for husbands who fail to gain custody of their children can appear intolerable. Attempts to remove such children from their mothers and to return them to be brought up in their father's country of origin are not uncommon.

The welfare principle can be difficult to apply in the case of children of mixed and of purely Asian origin. The influences to which they are exposed can raise in them expectations with regard to their upbringing which may be unacceptable in their parents' eyes. How these expectations, which would be seen almost as a right in the case of English children, can be balanced against the need not to deprive them of the cultural heritage of their parents, is an acutely sensitive problem. Where indeed does the welfare of the child lie when these prove incompatible? Access, especially in mixed marriages, may appear at first sight to offer some compromises, but the practical arrangements all too often prove most difficult either to agree or to implement.

Religion

Western society is broadly based upon the Christian ethic and there remains an underlying assumption that the standards which it advocates still provide the 'proper' basis for both marriage and the upbringing of children. With active religious observance now the exception rather than the rule, the number of cases in which religious upbringing is a live issue are relatively few, but in its broadest conception it will still underpin many custody decisions. This explains in part why concepts of 'good' and 'bad' partners, as opposed to 'good' or 'bad' parents still hold some small sway, in the face of theories of child care which are not religiously based.

While courts may thus continue to give some weight to the

generalized concept of a Christian upbringing, they will usually and understandably be reluctant to become involved in issues which are effectively between different religious denominations. This must be so if society's expressions of religious toleration are not to be threatened by individual and personal judgements. The only possible exception concerns some of the more extreme religious sects whose influence, other than among those who choose to practice them, may be seen to be at variance with or even inimical towards the general cultural expectation. The proposed imposition of a rigid and intolerant religious upbringing which might serve to isolate a child either from his absent parent or from the community at large must be a factor for the court to weigh in a custody decision. Even then, however, it remains a question of conscience which must be approached with no little circumspection.

CONCILIATION IN CUSTODY ISSUES

Disputes over custody are more understandable in the layman's eyes than those over access, because the desire to continue to care for one's children after divorce is generally recognized as a natural extension of the feelings which go to make up a 'good' parent. Insofar as parents are unlikely to abandon their cause without a fight, the opportunities for conciliation work which leads directly to a consent order are comparatively few. Yet paradoxical as it may seem, contested custody issues do not as a rule provoke the same bitter antagonism and sense of perpetuated conflict as disputes over access.

This is partly because the contest over custody does not always carry the connotations of emotional disturbance and almost of fighting for its own sake which are common in the access situation. Parents are on the whole more willing to concede the good faith of the party who opposes them. Another factor is the clear-cut nature of the decision which the court has to make: one parent at least emerges from the proceedings with what he set out to achieve.

This is not to suggest that the conciliation function is any less important in custody issues. It is rather that its effects are less likely to influence the outcome of the application before the court, but it can still help parents and children to live more happily with the decision. It can in the process also reduce the likelihood of further proceedings.

Conciliation with the Custodial Parent

It may seem at first sight that there is little work which remains to be done with the parent whose application is successful since he is presumably well satisfied with the outcome. In practice, continued contact often proves beneficial. Much as the welfare officer may have attempted to dissuade the parties from too crudely a partisan approach to the proceedings, first reactions after the event will still often be of having won. Accompanying them at times will be an assumption that the court has by its decision conferred the accolade of being the 'better' parent. The feeling that justice has prevailed may carry demeaning and derogatory messages to and about the other parent, which can lead to serious future difficulties over access. It is in the weeks immediately following the hearing that inappropriate notions of superiority should be identified, examined and discarded.

A further reason for the continued contact is that the euphoria produced by a successful application may prove surprisingly short lived. The practicalities of caring for the children, whether in a single parent family or in all the complexities of a reconstituted unit, can be much more demanding than was anticipated in the essentially emotional battle for their possession. The long term realities and responsibilities loom large quite abruptly once the issue is settled. Feelings of inadequacy can surface with unexpected suddenness and many doubts and fears are better shared than dwelt upon unproductively. The conciliation task here is the familiar one of helping the parent to reach a realistic evaluation of his situation and of rebuilding his self-image so that he is properly reassured as to the capabilities which both the court and the welfare officer have discerned in him.

Conciliation with the Absent Parent

The help that a parent needs when he is left without the custody of his children is at the same time more easy to recognize and more difficult to provide. The feelings of worthlessness produced by the divorce will have been reinforced and he will see himself not only as a failed marriage partner but as a failed parent as well. In apparent conflict with this overriding sense of failure, there will often be a deeply felt sense of anger and of injustice. This will constitute a necessary part of his immediate defences, as he rejects as 'wrong' a decision whose implications he is not yet able to face up to and accept.

There are several possible objectives of counselling and, since loss of self-esteem is a common response, reappraisal of self and realistic rebuilding will figure prominently. Anger against the judicial machinery, which includes the welfare service, may have to be allowed free rein until it can be first contained, then examined for its validity, and finally accepted as a legitimate but intermediate response. There may be hostility towards the successful parent and even towards the children for being happy in his care; again, understanding must come before acceptance of their attitudes and indeed of their happiness.

To understand and accept why the court has decided in favour of the other parent is a major step towards attempting to make that decision workable for the children rather than seeking to frustrate its operation through access difficulties. From here it is perhaps possible to move forward to contemplating and then planning a life which does not include the children on a full-time basis. This is the key to reintegration in society as a divorced and non-custodial parent. There can never be full compensation for the loss of family – and loss it is, however well access may work – and this too must be acknowledged and accepted. The objective must be a refashioned life which includes the children positively but which does not, other than in response to their manifest need, seek physically to repossess them. It calls for a high level of understanding of self, partner and children, and for a considerable measure of unselfishness and self discipline; it will not often be achieved alone.

The task of conciliation with the absent parent tends too often to be neglected unless and until his problems force attention, usually because of difficulties over access. Valuable time is lost whilst attitudes are hardening, and the work is made incomparably more difficult. The absent parent may all too often be justified in feeling that he was rejected as a person along with his unsuccessful custody claim, and that the welfare officer is now concerned less with his feelings as an individual than with achieving a peaceable solution to the problems he is creating. His greatest need is immediately after the hearing, when the hurt is most acute and feelings of worthlessness are at their height. It is true that his anger will also then be at its height, and the welfare officer may be seen as a legitimate target for it if the court has followed a specific recommendation. But if involvement at this stage is threatening for the welfare officer, it is a responsibility which is nonetheless implicit in his role.

4

Access

An order made for the custody of a child in divorce proceedings will normally include a provision for his absent parent to have access to him. This provision is based upon the generally accepted view that, unless it offends against his overall interest, the child has the right to grow up knowing and maintaining contact with both his parents, despite the fact of their divorce. Access is not, as is often supposed, an inherent right of the absent parent, since the doctrine that the welfare of the child is paramount may on occasion constitute a bar.

Access has no independent legal standing on its own. Divorced parents can and often do make unsanctioned arrangements, but where access is formally granted by the court it can only be as an adjunct to a custody order. The court, in allowing access, may attach no conditions, leaving the parties to work out their own arrangements under the blanket provision of 'reasonable access', or it can define the frequency, duration and location of the contact between the child and his absent parent. This definition can differentiate between 'visiting access' during which the child sees the absent parent only for a day or part of a day and 'staying access' during which he stops for a week-end or longer period at the parent's home, or goes on holiday with him.

THE LEGAL PROVISION

Reasonable Access

The provision for reasonable access is based upon the assumption that two parents, although divorced, can retain some degree of insight into the continuing needs of their children and can approach the question of access with some measure of objectivity. It assumes that they will be able to reach agreement as to the best arrangement for maintaining contact between the children and their absent parent. This provision is all that is needed in the majority of cases; reasonable access, working reasonably well, is the rule rather than the exception. It is important for the welfare officer to remember this if he is to keep a proper sense of proportion. The more intractable problems with which he is regularly engaged do in fact represent only a small fraction of the total of access situations.

Defined Access

The court can be called upon to define access if the parties, although accepting that it should take place in principle, are unable to reach agreement as to the details of the arrangements, or differ as to the desirability of allowing staying as well as visiting access. Should the court decide to grant access against the wishes of the custodial parent, definition will almost certainly be necessary since agreement as to terms in this situation will be virtually impossible.

Disputes as to the most suitable definition of access are most common when children are still young. Too frequent or prolonged a contact with the absent parent may be held to be confusing and distressing if they are unable fully to understand their parents' new situation. Too brief or too infrequent a contact, on the other hand, may be seen as denying the absent parent the opportunity to establish any lasting or worthwhile relationship. Hard and fast rules, or even rough and ready guide lines, are impossible to lay down. Each case must be judged on its individual merits, with the best interests of the children rather than the wishes or convenience of the parents as the determining factor.

Older and more articulate children are likely to have opinions of their own and definition in their case will as a rule pose fewer problems. Whilst their views should not be allowed to determine the issue completely, they will have to be accorded some weight, and the stage is certainly reached by the time they are in their teens where definition in terms which are wholly unacceptable to them will present formidable problems of enforcement.

Access as a Legal Remedy

The determination of disputes over access is singularly ill-suited to the judicial process as we know it. The adversarial system upon which it is based has been identified too closely and for too long with the concepts of winning and losing for it to be able to adapt with comfort to the process of conciliation which, as is becoming increasingly recognized, is the only satisfactory method of dealing with access problems. The institution of legal proceedings leads all too often to a polarization of the positions of the parties, with the focus concentrated on their differences to the neglect of such common ground as may exist. There is too little facility for making use of the common ground as a platform for constructive negotiation.

When a court decides that access should be permitted against the wishes of the child or the custodial parent there are all too many ways in which it can be rendered ineffectual, and the possible sanctions are both few and largely inappropriate (see pages 72–5). Similarly, when access is formally defined, the parent or child who is determined to circumvent the order will invariably find some means of doing so. To be effective access requires the goodwill and working cooperation of the child and both his parents, and for this it is impossible to legislate. Many judges are coming to accept that their effective powers in relation to access are limited and they are demonstrating a marked reluctance to force upon unwilling parents and children specific requirements which are manifestly repugnant to them. They are instead becoming increasingly disposed to allow for access in principle by making an order for reasonable access, but to leave the practical problems of implementation in the hands of a supervising welfare officer (see page 68).

The Right of the Child

Section 52(1) of the Matrimonial Causes Act 1973 provides that 'custody in relation to a child includes access to the child'. From this it follows that judges, in determining questions of access, must be guided by the same welfare principle which obtains in custody issues. This, it will be recalled, is stated in Section 1 of the Guardianship of Minors Act 1971 which requires that 'the court . . . shall regard the welfare of the minor as the first and paramount consideration'. It has been seen that this principle is strictly adhered to in matters of custody and that decisions would not be affected materially in practice if the welfare of the child were to be made the absolute test. The position becomes somewhat different when it is access which is in dispute; the same statement could not then be made with equal confidence.

It might be expected, even on the test of welfare as 'the first and paramount consideration' that the court's initial approach would, as far as possible, be one of objective neutrality: an attempt to determine without any preconceived ideas whether it is in the interests of this particular child for access to be allowed in these particular circumstances. This is not in fact the case. There is usually a very powerful initial assumption that access is to be desired and a demand for the most compelling of evidence before the possibility of refusing it is considered. The onus is placed squarely upon the parent who is seeking to deny access and it is for him to demonstrate that it would be harmful to the child. Yet logically it could be argued that the position should be reversed. It is, after all, the applicant parent who is asking the court to make a positive order and an order, moreover, which will require the child's active cooperation if it is to be effective. Perhaps he should at least have to prove his case, rather than have its assumed merits taken for granted.

Three judgments in the Court of Appeal in access issues serve to demonstrate that whilst greater recognition has been given to the welfare principle in recent years, the courts are still nonetheless extremely conservative in their approach to the possibility of denying access. In the first of these, S v S (1962), it was stated:

> In the ordinary way that (i.e. access) would be no more than the basic right of any parent . . . to deprive a mother of access to her own children is a very strong thing to do . . . the court should not take that step unless satisfied that she is not a fit and proper person to be brought into contact with the children at all.

The emphasis here is essentially upon the 'right' of a suitable parent to have access to her children. The implications in terms of the welfare of the children, provided that the parent is suitable to have access, are effectively ignored.

Matters move forward in B v B (1971), in which a 16 year old boy is unwilling to see his father, but the Court's anxieties over denying access, albeit in his best interests, are very clear:

> For a court to deprive a parent completely of access to his child is to make a dreadful order .... Very seldom can the court bring itself to make so draconian an order and rarely is it necessary .... There is now no suggestion in the present case that the father is in any way an unfit person to have access to this boy. But, putting it the other way round the boy is not, in his frame of mind, a suitable person to have access to his father .... It cannot do him any good, and might very well do him harm.

The principle of the welfare of the child is taken as the test, and the 'right' of the suitable parent to have access is not upheld where these two demands conflict.

The issue is crystalized in M v M (1973), an appeal against an order discontinuing a mother's access on the grounds that it had proved detrimental to the child:

> the companionship of a parent is in any ordinary circumstances of such immense value to the child that there is a basic right in him to such companionship. I for my part would prefer to call it a basic right in the child rather than a basic right in the parent. That only means this, that no court should deprive a child of access to either parent unless it is wholly satisfied that access should cease and that is a conclusion at which a court should be extremely slow to arrive.

The apparent contradiction of the idea of 'a basic right in the child' with 'the basic right of any parent' in S v S and similar cases is explained as follows:

> They mean and are meant to mean not that any parent has a proprietorial right to access, but that save in exceptional circumstances to deprive a parent of access is to deprive a child of an important contribution to his emotional and material growing up in the long term.

The concept of a parent's 'right' to access is here discounted in any formal legal sense and the 'right' is vested in the child.

The court is, however, starting from the assumption that access can, as a general rule, be confidently expected to be to the child's advantage.

Whilst it is certainly true that good access, working well, is beneficial to the majority of children, the 'exceptional circumstances' in which access can properly be denied probably occur more frequently than these various observations would seem to imply. The court does accept, in M v M, that the point can be reached at which access ceases to be beneficial and should therefore be terminated. It is at least possible that in their anxiety not to deprive children of the benefits of good access, judges are too reluctant to refuse or to terminate it when a strict application of the welfare principle makes this desirable. It is possible too that the 'right' of the deserving parent does still carry more weight than ought to be the case.

THE EMOTIONAL CONTEXT

It is a common mistake among inexperienced practitioners in the welfare field to assume that access, involving as it does only an occasional contact between parent and child, should present fewer problems than custody, where nothing less than the permanent physical possession of the child is at stake. In practice, this rarely proves to be the case, since the problems to which access gives rise both in human and in welfare terms are by far the more complex. One reason for this is that access does not lend itself to the clear-cut 'either/or' decision of the custody dispute, the variations and graduations of defined access, both visiting and staying, being almost infinite.

The Parents

One of the most striking characteristics of access disputes is that both parents usually tend to see themselves as the only losers and to regard their former partners as being unreasonably selfish or awkward in refusing to comply with their wishes. To some extent these attitudes are understandable. The mother who has custody may well complain that it is she who has to deal with the problems of sickness and of discipline and with the inevitable trauma caused by parental separation; that it is she in fact who has to cope with all the stressful and unattractive aspects of child-rearing, only to have her efforts undermined by the spoiling and disruptive influence of the pseudo-Father Christmas figure who appears on alternate Sunday afternoons. Power without responsibility indeed! The father in such a situation may complain with equal bitterness that the mother who enjoys her child's company for 13½ days in 14 without interruption, a condition to which he would dearly love to aspire, is graceless enough to complain because he and the child do manage to achieve a few hours of uninhibited enjoyment together.

Each parent in this caricatured situation has a legitimate if extremely stated point of view. Each of them is seeing it exclusively from his or her own standpoint, without thought for the difficulties which the other is facing. The scene is thus set for confrontation, with each convinced of the justice of his or her own cause and already persuaded that the other is activated only by malice or sheer bloody-mindedness, or probably a combination of both. The absence of any mention of the children's needs in this situation is not an oversight: such considerations will all too probably have been submerged beneath the parents' quarrel.

Second Partners

If parents on their own can have problems over access, the position becomes even more complex when either of them enters into a second marriage or domestic relationship. The emotional responses of both parents and children to this event will vary enormously according to individual circumstances, but it is safe to predict that few of them will be wholly positive. It will be particularly unwelcome to the former spouse who has not or does not wish to contract any similar liaison. The heightened feelings of failure and of worthlessness which are engendered will usually be expressed in terms of disapproval of the new partner.

If the second partner has been directly involved in the events leading up to the marriage breakdown, the disapproval will be obvious and specific in its manifestations. It will be expressed with the most vehemence when the second partner was known to both the parties before the liaison began; this is as sure a recipe as any for access problems. Even when he or she is newly come upon the scene and was not involved prior to the marriage breakdown, the fact of being replaced and of therefore being finally cast off must always be to a greater or lesser extent unpalatable.

It is rare indeed for these negative feelings not to be transmitted at least in part to the children of the family. The potential, so far as access is concerned, will inevitably be for ill rather than for good.

The Children

Any dispute over access puts pressure upon the loyalties and emotions of the children. The knowledge that their parents are in conflict over them – a fact which cannot be concealed from any but the very young – is likely to leave them confused and distressed even when they have only their own natural parents to contend with.

For them, too, the position becomes much more complex when second partners are introduced. There are new relationships to be learnt, not only with the new partner and his or her children, but possibly with a new extended family as well. This process can never be an easy one, containing as it must feelings of no little ambivalence towards many of the people involved. The new partner may be identified as the cause of the marriage breakdown and be resented accordingly. Even when not viewed in this manner, he or she will still be seen as a usurper and as a potential rival for those affections still properly reserved for the natural mother or father. Any child whom the second partner brings to the new family unit must likewise be seen as a rival, this time for the affection of the parent into whose home he has been introduced. The dependability and whole-hearted affection of this parent will then become suspect in its turn, since he is apparently willing to share his love beyond the boundaries of his original family.

The adjustments demanded of the child are formidable even when the new relationship is contracted by the parent with whom he is living. Here, however, he does at least have the advantage of continuous contact and there is usually some implicit acceptance of a quasi-parenting role on the part of the second partner. His problems will be more acute when a new liaison is formed by his absent parent, with whom his access meetings provide but a poor substitute for living together. The new relationship may well seem to have confirmed his original feelings of rejection and the new partner will be a largely unknown quantity, whose sense of commitment to him has yet to be put to the test. This is not to suggest that the new partner of an absent parent may not have much to offer to the child in the access relationship or that he or she can never be accepted or indeed ultimately loved. The fact remains, however, that the pattern of relationships and of the child's responses to them becomes very much more complex, and the tensions attendant in many access situations can be greatly increased in consequence.

Staying Access

Proposals for staying access, for the child to spend a night or a week-end or a longer period at the home of his absent parent, are often the cause of heated and highly emotional disputes, particularly in the case of young children. The custodial parent will frequently feel acutely threatened, often fearing that the child will be influenced against him, or even not returned at all.

It is suggested on occasion that it is the only feasible arrangement because the two homes are too far apart for visiting access to be practical on a frequent and regular basis. This type of argument ignores the question of the child's wishes and welfare, and the factor of distance alone is not sufficient to justify its implementation.

More cogently, perhaps, it can be argued that prolonged stays at the home of the absent parent, or holidays taken with him, will help him to foster a more natural and sustained relationship than is possible on a visiting basis. Against this it may be held that too long a separation from the custodial parent causes unnecessary anxiety and distress to younger children. The provision of adequate physical care may be called into question, especially where the absent parent is the father. If he should have a second partner to assist him in looking after the children, doubts may be cast upon her suitability to come into contact with them. Similar objections may of course be made to the second partner of an absent mother.

Many disputes over staying access arise against this background of second partners and they can be exacerbated when, as is often the case, children have been influenced by the custodial parents against them. When children do experience genuine feelings of antipathy against a second partner, the question of staying access should be approached with caution, as the case of Patricia demonstrates:

> Patricia's parents had separated some three months previously, when her mother left the matrimonial home to live with another man in a town some 200 miles to the north. Patricia, the oldest at 14 of five children, had borne the brunt of her father's initial hurt and bewilderment and of his subsequent vitriolic hostility towards his wife and especially towards her cohabitee. Problems of distance and of finance effectively precluded visiting access, but before matters reached court father arranged, on his solicitor's advice, for a week's staying access; he had been assured that no court would deny his wife this measure of contact with her children. Five highly unwilling children were duly transported north, but Patricia, having by now thoroughly internalized her father's attitudes, ran away within 24 hours and attempted to hitch hike home.

That Patricia came to no harm was entirely fortuitous. The fact was that her father had been ill advised. This was clearly an inappropriate time at which to attempt to impose staying access, and the failure to consider the strength of feeling in a highly emotional and upset adolescent was a major oversight. An order for staying access, after proper investigations had been made, would scarcely have been the likely outcome. The episode illustrates, too, the sound general principle that enforced staying access is unlikely to resolve problems between the child and parent or child and second partner if reasonable relationships have not already been established through visiting access.

One is not seeking through this example to suggest that staying access is in general undesirable. It has, on the contrary, much to commend it in appropriate circumstances. It enables an absent parent to depart from the role of an indulgent visitor and to experience at first hand some of the problems of catering continuously for a child in circumstances in which his behaviour may well be more difficult and demanding. It can at the same time provide the custodial parent with a much-needed break from the pressures, if such they be, of living as a single parent family. It does call for a greater measure of tolerance and trust on the part of the custodial parent – fears that the holiday will prove to be the thin edge of the wedge which will ultimately seduce the child's affections on a permanent basis are often felt and do not always prove groundless. The advantages to the child, however, can be enormous. Provided he is not pressed to make any greater commitment than he feels able to give, he can continue to enjoy the comforting assurance of a secure and loving relationship with both parents.

CONCILIATION

Access problems tend to be most acute in those cases where one or both parents have unresolved difficulties in relation to their former marriage. Access cannot begin to work satisfactorily until these difficulties have at least been recognized and it is in helping parents to face up to and accept their divorced status that the welfare officer becomes engaged in the conciliation process.

Parents in Conflict

Parents continue in conflict after divorce when one or both of them fails in some measure to accept that their marriage is at an end. The legal tie has been broken, but the emotional chains remain. The failure to adjust may be the result of one parent still wishing, though usually at an unconscious level, for the marriage to continue. Alternatively, the still unresolved problems may produce in one or both the need to continue to fight out unfinished battles in a bitter and hostile but still quasi-marital relationship.

In such situations the children of the marriage may offer the last available battleground and they often become the focus of their parents' continuing hostilities. To describe them as pawns in the game is a well worn cliche, but as with most cliches it has its element of truth. The majority of parents who use their children in this way do not do so as a matter of deliberate policy, being willing to see them hurt, as hurt they must be, in the process. The odd exception does occur, but not with anything like the frequency that many a struggling and embattled access applicant would believe. These parents are, on the contrary, so caught up with their own hurts and their own problems and so convinced as to the justice of their own cause that the possibility of their behaviour being to their children's disadvantage simply does not occur to them.

The Child as a Focus of Conflict

The child caught up in the bitterness and hatred of this kind of conflict has his own peculiar problems which make him most difficult to help. They also make it more than usually difficult for an enquiring welfare officer to establish what he really wants at all. Having witnessed the traumatic effects of the marriage breakdown, with all the connotations of bereavement and of rejection which this implies, and having perhaps taken to himself as well quite inappropriate feelings of responsibility and therefore of guilt for what has occurred, his most demanding need will almost certainly be for the demonstrable love and security which his remaining parent can provide. It is hard enough to persuade any child that he is still allowed to love the departed parent; even when he is provided with a secure and accepting environment in which the absent parent is presented in positive terms, it may be weeks or months before he finds the confidence to commit himself effectively in the new relationship. How much more difficult then is the position of the child who is not only denied the opportunity to readjust the focus of his relationships from this kind of secure base, but who is also actively discouraged from maintaining any kind of contact with his absent parent. His need for acceptance and security from his remaining parent is imperative. When this is made effectively conditional upon his rejection of the absent parent, it is hardly surprising that he should only rarely discover the strength and the determination to resist.

Such a child is Roberta.

Roberta's mother had originally been granted the custody of all three of her children, of whom Roberta is the youngest. Her older son and daughter had each opted in their early teens to live with father and his second wife. They had done so largely because of her implacable opposition to any form of access. Although not without affection for their mother, they had found the restraints she sought to impose intolerable and had ultimately chosen to live in their father's more relaxed and relatively stress-free home. Their plans to enjoy a fuller relationship with both parents from this base had come to nothing: bitterly hurt by their rejection of her, mother had spurned all their subsequent overtures and access in the reverse direction had also proved effectively unworkable.

Mother now has Roberta as the sole audience for her vituperation against her former husband. He has not only abandoned her for another woman, but has also, in her eyes, seduced the older children away from her as well. She clings to her younger daughter with a fierce and unreasoning possessiveness, determined that she shall not be allowed to desert her. The obvious method of prevention is to deny the child all contact with her father and this she achieves not by any formal refusal to allow access to take place, but by making it abundantly clear that Roberta will forfeit her love should she choose to participate.

For eight year old Roberta the problem is insoluble. She has, in the welfare officer's estimation, no serious objection to visiting father, with whom she has been observed to be on reasonably cordial terms; her pleasure at seeing her brother and sister again has been unmistakable. To admit even this much, however, would be to bring down upon herself the very considerable wrath which she has already seen visited upon her brother and sister in similar circumstances. She has, in any case, a close and affectionate relationship with her mother, and having witnessed her acute distress over the previous departures, she is understandably unwilling to take what her mother assures her would be the first step in the same direction. Not surprisingly, the child opts out.

The court's order for fortnightly access lies disregarded. Mother is tacitly inviting father to seek his remedy by means of penal sanctions and she leaves her daughter in no doubt as to the court's powers in this respect. The thought that her father might ultimately seek to secure her mother's imprisonment does little to enhance his image in Roberta's eyes, although it heightens her anxieties still further. It encourages her, too, to share her mother's contempt for the court and its agents and to see the welfare officer, as she does, as an enforcement officer briefed to secure for father his legal rights, regardless of the merits of his case. With no one in whom she can safely confide, she has no option but to comply with her mother's wishes, and this she continues stolidly and consistently to do.

Whether or not Roberta would choose to see her father had she any genuine freedom in the matter has become relatively unimportant. The only certainty is that in the existing emotional climate the order for access is not realistically enforceable.

The Role of the Welfare Officer

The conciliator

The case of Roberta illustrates very well the importance of the welfare officer's role as conciliator in access issues. He had here realized at an early stage that the central difficulty did not lie with Roberta, whose attitudes towards her father and towards the whole question of access were well within the boundaries of conventionally accepted and acceptable response. He had correctly identified the mother's extreme and even irrational attitudes as the principal area of difficulty and had properly chosen them as the focus for his case work effort. Without attempting to work through the whole history of the failed marriage, he had nonetheless acquired a sufficient understanding of it to be able to place those attitudes in a comprehensible context. He had thereafter tried to help the mother achieve some measure of insight, upon which an attempted modification of her hitherto impenetrable intransigence could be based. Diagnosis, as is so often the case, proved easier than treatment and little progress was achieved. He was, as he ultimately came to realize, dealing with a woman whose emotional need to continue in a state of conflict with her former husband was so great as to override all other considerations.

Failure by the welfare officer in the role of conciliator spells almost certain disaster so far as any resolution of access difficulties is concerned. Where both welfare officers and judges are most likely to be in error is in seeking to battle on with situations where conciliation has been attempted and has failed. The truly intractable cases should be recognized as such. There is all too often a Micawberish tendency to wait and to hope on the flimsiest of foundations for something to turn up, instead of bringing matters to a swift and clean conclusion and terminating access if this is what the welfare of the child demands. Pointless persistence in a cause which is already lost is more likely to add to than to ameliorate his difficulties.

The reporter

The problems which the welfare officer faces in these complicated situations are heightened by the limited time span within which he frequently has to work. The contested access issue, viewed objectively, does seem to offer an ideal opportunity for intensive casework intervention on a short-term basis. The six to eight week period conventionally allotted to the task does nonetheless seem at times to be pathetically brief. Extensions can be sought and will normally be granted, but in many cases this is not appropriate. The anxieties which the conflict produces in the child will often demand that the formal court proceedings be disposed of as rapidly as possible.

If the welfare officer can, despite this limitation, help the parties to arrive at a solution which is acceptable to them both and consistent with the child's interests, the matter in court can proceed without contest by means of a consent order. This is probably one of the most useful functions he can perform. He must nonetheless proceed with caution. He must not pressurize the parties to the point where they feel that they have been denied a full and open hearing and neither must he trespass too far upon the specific decision-making area which is the province of the court alone.

When he finds it impossible to bring the parties to an agreed solution, it remains open to the welfare officer to advise the court if he feels that any specific definition would be in the child's best interests. In the nature of things, it must be that any such proposal will be more acceptable to one parent than to the other. The feeling that he is prejudiced in favour of that parent will often be keenly experienced by the other and it is therefore essential for him to spell out as clearly as possible the thinking which underlies his recommendation. He is dealing, however, in a highly emotional area where hopes and expectations are not always rationally based, and it by no means follows that his objective and theoretically-based assessment will prove acceptable to the parent who feels himself to be aggrieved. He is left therefore with at least one disgruntled parent and with the uneasy knowledge that there is more work yet to be done if he is to prevent this residual dissatisfaction from spilling over into renewed access problems.

Repercussions of this kind following a specific recommendation as to the desirable terms of access can make the conciliation task with the reluctant parent much more demanding in the period after the court hearing. The parent who feels that his position has been effectively pre-empted by the court's decision is less likely to prove amenable than the one who feels that his opinions are still being considered and that he still has some influence on events. Thus whilst definition may be inevitable in some circumstances, too detailed an order may create as many problems as it solves. Where the welfare officer feels that there is any hope at all of gaining the parent's cooperation, a better order is for reasonable access together with a supervision order, with the implementation of access and the detailed arrangements to be at the discretion of the supervising officer. Some judges, it is true, are reluctant to put such power into social work rather than judicial hands, but if conciliation is to be the aim, an order of this kind probably offers the best prospect of ultimate success.

ENFORCEMENT OF ACCESS

The problems of disputed access do not, as has already been suggested, lend themselves very readily to resolution through the legal process. This is because they are in essence social and emotional problems rather than legal ones. It is not therefore surprising that the courts should be faced with peculiar difficulties when parents or children fail to comply with orders for access. The available sanctions are inevitably legal ones and as such they are in general both too severe and too inflexible to offer any hope of dealing effectively with the situations which they are called upon to rectify.

The fact that courts tend to be over cautious in their approach to the possibility of denying access, and attempt at times to enforce orders which from a social work point of view are effectively unworkable, does little to ease the position. A further factor is that, whilst it is problematic enough to deal with recalcitrant parents in this very emotional area, it is virtually impossible to cater for the child who refuses to conform.

The Unwilling Child

Access is only refused by the courts in exceptional circumstances and the reluctance of a child to see his absent parent is not generally held of itself to be a sufficient reason for denying it. This view is held the more strongly when there is reason to believe that indoctrination by the custodial parent has contributed significantly to his attitude. The desire to secure for even an unwilling child the theoretical benefits of contact with an eminently suitable absent parent and to negate the indoctrination of a deliberately vengeful spouse is wholly understandable, but such an approach pays too little heed to the principle that the child's welfare is paramount. If access or the prospect of it is genuinely disturbing to a child, his interests will hardly be served by a judicial insistence that it be pursued regardless of his feelings. The concept of indoctrination is irrelevant: what matters is his present state of mind and the effect which access would have upon him. This will be the same no matter how his present attitude was brought about. His welfare in such circumstances may well demand that access be refused, even if his attitude is specifically attributable to the influence of his custodial parent. This is well illustrated by the case of Margaret.

> Margaret is a pretty and intelligent nine year old, the only child of her mother's late and disastrous marriage to a cultured and capable West African doctor. She is very well cared for physically and has a warm and loving relationship with her mother. Her mother has considerable emotional problems, not least over her own mixed marriage, and, secure in a different town, she is bringing her daughter up as white. She has nothing but contempt for father's second wife, another English woman, whom she considers to be her social inferior. Nominally she does not oppose access, provided that there is no contact with the second wife, but she does nothing to facilitate it. Margaret's comments to the

effect that 'daddy cannot love me because he left me' remain unchallenged, as also do her vehement objections to being seen locally with 'a black man'.

The prospect of access makes Margaret physically ill. On several occasions she has such violent attacks of vomiting that the meeting has to be cancelled. Mother soothes her ills, whilst railing against the inhumanity of the court which has insisted upon access, and condemning the man who deliberately brings such suffering on his child. Systematically, she reinforces the child's fears of access and, by extension, of her father.

The welfare officer knows that father has much to offer his daughter in theory. He would be able to help her come to terms with her mixed racial origins and would broaden her horizons in many respects beyond the narrow and inward-looking suburban gentility with which her mother is slowly stifling her. It is clear, too, that the mother is creating many a future problem for Margaret in passing on her own bitter and cynical attitudes towards men and marriage and that father's influence here would again be beneficial. All this knowledge is useless since events are dictated by the extreme nature of the child's reactions. The virtual certainty that the child's attitudes are mother-induced is of no help either. The possibility of transferring custody from the mother who has cherished her all her life to the father whom she now hardly knows and of whom she has been taught to be afraid cannot seriously be contemplated. For her to continue in her present state of stress, sickness and apprehension is equally intolerable. The only solution, despite all that her father could so willingly offer her, is to terminate the access arrangement.

To Margaret's father the proposal to end access altogether seemed like a denial of fundamental justice, and from his own narrow point of view it could be described as such. Access, however, is not concerned with justice to deserving parents, but with the interests and welfare of their children: to lose sight of this fundamental fact is to lose contact with what it is or should be about. It is almost to ask the impossible of such a father, who is not responsible for its failure, to refrain nonetheless from seeking for its enforcement. It is no surprise that such parents should continue to fight for what they see as justice, even though each succeeding legal battle may serve only to drive the loved and wanted child even further away. Attempted enforcement through the courts cannot, in the end, provide a solution which satisfies anyone.

The view that the child's wishes alone are not a sufficient reason for denying access can present formidable practical problems when he literally refuses to comply with the order which the court has made. How much pressure can the custodial parent reasonably be expected to exert in the face of a point blank refusal to cooperate? Should it, in the last resort, take the form of physical compulsion, with the child carried bodily to the meeting place? Or if he is too big to be taken against his wishes, what then? It is tempting to dismiss such methods as wholly unthinkable and yet the question cannot be begged so easily. Some desperate custodial parents have been forced to such measures because of the assumption, on occasion clearly stated by courts, that if they are unable to persuade or coerce their children into compliance, their competence and suitability as custodians will be called seriously into question. In fact, of course, the disturbed and hysterically refusing child will often not be amenable to the controls which a normally competent parent can easily exercise in other contexts. This is not yet sufficiently understood. Until the depths of feeling and determination which even small children can display are more widely appreciated, inappropriate and potentially damaging attempts at legally sanctioned enforcement will continue to be made.

The Unwilling Parent

Many experienced welfare officers hold the view that enforcement of an access order is in the end impossible if the custodial parent is determined to resist it. The methods of evasion which are employed are often of a kind which are not susceptible to proof or disproof in a strictly legal sense, and the attitude or the emotional condition of the child on any individual occasion can be adduced as reasons for postponing the ordered meetings almost indefinitely. This is in many ways more insidious in its effects than when the parent adopts a 'damm the consequences' attitude and prepares for outright confrontation. The evasive approach, if it may be so termed, develops all too often into a war of attrition, with the possibility of further court proceedings hanging like a threatening cloud, and all the parties in a state of perpetual tension as they wait for the storm to break. It takes little imagination to appreciate the effect on the child, be he for access or against it, as he watches the conflict develop between his parents and waits for the clash which he can neither influence nor prevent.

The openly challenging parent, who in effect defies the court to do its worst, exposes the limitations of our present system to the full, since there is no effective way of dealing with him. There are only two practical sanctions available. The first is imprisonment for contempt of the court's order and the second is the removal of the child from his control. In many cases neither will be appropriate, in which situation the court may be left with little alternative but to endorse, if only by default, his refusal to cooperate. This is clearly undesirable, since any order of the court should be seen to be enforceable, and it serves to emphasize yet again how inappropriate the legal setting is for the resolution of this kind of dispute.

Judicial Sanctions

The penal clause

The idea of invoking penal sanctions against an intransigent parent is one which most judges are understandably reluctant to entertain. The use of such powers in the regulation of family relationships is not only repugnant in itself, but is also all too often self-defeating. At best, the threat implicit in a penal clause (a formal endorsement on the order informing the parent that failure to comply with its requirements will constitute contempt of court and will render him liable to imprisonment) will secure an unwilling and unconvinced compliance; at worst, it will have to be put into practice. This will be bound to have a damaging effect on the child, who will not only lose one parent in acutely traumatic circumstances, but will almost certainly blame the other for what has happened. The hostility between the parents will be heightened unendurably and the child further distanced from both of them. The atmosphere created will hardly be conducive to a happy access relationship, if and when contact is resumed.

Nevertheless, while the provision for access remains within

the ambit of the civil law, which as a part of the provision for custody it surely must, the question of sanctions cannot be avoided. Unenforceable orders are by definition bad orders and the decisions of the court must at the last be seen to be binding. The welfare of the children in whose interests they are made demands nothing less. There may, perhaps, be more scope than is presently acknowledged for some form of intermediate action by the court, but there would seem to be no logical alternative to imprisonment as the ultimate sanction.

Given that the penal clause must remain within the armoury of the court, one would still hope to find it used on only the rarest of occasions. In the event, applications for its inclusion in orders for access are more common than might be supposed. In their least helpful form, they are made long before all other expedients have been exhausted. They then represent little more than a step in the adversarial process, a serving of notice, as it were, that the issue is to be contested with full vigour. Such applications, often made with little expectation of success and with the transparent intention of intimidating the 'opposition' almost from the outset, seem far less concerned with the child's welfare than with the pursuit of personal and often vindictive adult ends.

The court itself in dealing with applications will have regard for the welfare of the child, but it does not necessarily follow that all penal notices can be justified from a social work point of view. Some judges are more sensitive than others to the dignity of their position and are less sympathetic to any breach of their original orders. They may in consequence pay too little heed to the all important question of motivation, and fail to distinguish between the parent who seeks in good faith for a genuinely unpalatable remedy and the one who is motivated primarily by a desire for retribution against his former spouse. They may fail similarly to differentiate between the parent who tries honestly by his resistance to safeguard the interests of his child and the one who relies on the court's known reluctance to employ penal sanctions to pursue less praiseworthy ends with impunity. On some occasions at least, the manner in which a parent prosecutes his cause can seem to weigh more heavily than his reasons for undertaking it.

A final danger with the penal clause is that it may be introduced in an attempt to resolve an immediate impasse, without sufficient thought as to the consequences should it fail to achieve this objective. A parent may well persuade himself under the immediate pressure of the court proceedings that he will make the arrangements work, come what may. When faced with the reality of the situation, however, perhaps with a child whose cooperation is hysterically withheld, personal convictions as to what his welfare truly demands can easily override promises made in all good faith. The court is then in a dilemma. It cannot continue to admonish indefinitely, for the sanction would then become meaningless, but it may be equally unwilling to take the final step of committal if this would conflict with the best interests of the child. The only conclusion to be drawn is that courts should be very slow to attach penal notices in cases of this kind.

Reversal of custody

What amounts to an alternative sanction is the threat to the parent who refuses access to deny him the continued custody of his child should he persist in his refusal. Such a threat, made without reference to the welfare of the child, amounts to little more than direct coercion, in which the merits of the parent as a custodian are receiving neither recognition nor consideration, and as such it is wholly inappropriate.

This is not to suggest that the court, when satisfied that access is no longer a viable proposition, may not have to consider whether the interests of the child would not best be served in this new situation by a change of custody. The factors of personality, emotional stability and even mental health which lead a parent to so determined an opposition to access may also give rise to serious questioning as to whether he is indeed still fitted to have custody. This will not, however, be the case in every instance. There may be compelling factors against granting custody to a parent who is perfectly well suited to enjoy the access which he is presently being denied.

The personal qualities which help to promote satisfactory access are quite distinct from those required in a good custodial parent. It cannot be assumed that failure to conform in the one area implies a lack of suitability to continue in the other. It should be left to the parent who has been denied access to decide whether it is appropriate for him to apply for custody to be varied. He will certainly have given much thought as to whether it would be a practical proposition. If the court is in doubt in the absence of an application, it can always call for a welfare report. What it should not do is to raise the issue of its own volition, solely to secure an otherwise unobtainable acquiescence over access when the well-being of the child is not in question. This would seem to constitute a less than proper use of its powers.

SUPERVISED ACCESS

The court, in attempting to resolve difficult access problems, will on occasion order that access shall be supervised by the welfare officer. Argument is rife within the welfare service both as to whether such orders are valid in law and whether, when they are made, they can serve any useful purpose.

The Legal Authority

Section 42 of the Matrimonial Causes Act 1973 empowers the court to make 'such order as it thinks fit' for the custody and education of a child. The decision as to whether access shall be permitted and any necessary definition of its terms is provided for under the custody umbrella and 'such order as it thinks fit' would seem to be a general enough authority for the court to make whatever additional requirement may seem desirable. There would seem to be no reason in law why such an additional requirement should not be that access will take place under the supervision of a court welfare officer.

The Opposition to Supervised Access

The legal argument

It is held that if the time and place of access are defined, the court is in effect dictating to the supervising officer precisely when and where he shall carry out his duties. Such judicial intrusion into the daily working arrangements of the supervising agency is without precedent in any other form of statutory supervision. It is argued that the powers of the court extend only as far as ordering that there shall be supervised access, but that the details of its implementation are a matter only for the agency to whom the responsibility is entrusted. The weakness of this type of argument lies in its attempt to compare what are quite unlike forms of activity, although they share the generic title of supervision. Matrimonial supervision orders serve a quite different function from orders made in criminal or care proceedings. The powers of the supervising officer are different and the court can in fact employ different methods – such as supervised access – to secure the ends it desires.

Objections of this kind can in any event easily be overcome if the court is prepared to allow the welfare officer a sufficient degree of latitude in undertaking his task. An order that access shall take place under the supervision of the welfare officer and at such times and places as he shall determine, within a broad overall definition, would seem to dispose completely of the legal argument.

Its inappropriate use

Opposition to supervised access, although frequently couched in terms which question its legality, stems more from an unwillingness on the part of many officers to embark upon an emotionally fraught and very time-consuming operation for what they would see as a questionable advantage in social work terms. The fact that the exercise must usually be mounted at times of maximum inconvenience, including weekends and public holidays, does not add to its attractions. Above all, however, its opponents protest that it is used inappropriately, without consultation, and without any understanding or even consideration of what it entails.

It is unfortunately true that courts are still guilty of ordering supervised access without prior consultation and in circumstances in which it is clearly inappropriate. This can happen, for example, when lawyers are in sight of a consent order for custody but there are difficulties over access, which then becomes a bargaining counter. If one party is doubtful about allowing it, how better to solve the problem, they may think, than by having the access supervised by the welfare officer? This compromise is then pressed upon the parties and is endorsed by the court as a consent order, with the judge possibly quite unaware that the welfare service knows nothing of the arrangement. The welfare of the child has scarcely been considered in the search for a swift conclusion and the nature of supervised access, with all its limitations, has not been taken into account at all.

Its artificiality

Access, other than prolonged staying access, is always artificial. Supervised access is, by its nature, even less natural. One may reasonably question whether even the fondest of parents can respond spontaneously to his child in the presence of a third party, and especially when that third party is an official observer appointed by the court. The supervising officer, with the choice of taking no part in the proceedings at all, although he is manifestly not invisible, or of attempting to involve himself in what is an intensely personal and private relationship, is on the horns of no small dilemma. Actively or passively, he is the unwilling catalyst at a meeting which would clearly be otherwise but for his presence. The emotional imposition of this intrusion would be difficult to overstate, and those who maintain that it can never be justified and that its inherent artificiality negates whatever value it might otherwise have, do have a tenable point of view.

One would not agree that supervised access is defensible in the long term, or in other than certain specific and closely defined circumstances. One would maintain, however, that it can be justified, as always, when it is to the demonstrable advantage of the child. The circumstances in which such advantage does exist are now considered.

Supervised Access as a Means of Evaluation

In the context of evaluation, supervised access represents little more than an extension of what should in any event be the welfare officer's conventional pattern of enquiry. He cannot expect to report adequately upon a contested issue without seeing the child with the parent whose access is in dispute. Artificial as the arrangement may be, two or three meetings should enable him to begin to assess some of the qualities of the parent–child relationship and to assist the court in its decision in the light of what he has observed.

This method of enquiry is not possible unless both parents and children are prepared to offer their cooperation. When the children alone are the unwilling parties, the setting up of a supervised meeting will conveniently test out the strength of their refusal. Should it emerge that this is genuine and deep seated and that persistence with access would be distressing to them, the welfare officer may well conclude at an early stage that it would be unwise to press matters further. In this case it will have been established at the enquiry stage that a formal order for supervised access would be of little value.

The situation is very different when a seemingly willing child is being prevented, either by direct refusal or by indirect emotional pressure, from seeing his absent parent. Here the welfare officer is being denied the opportunity to observe and to report upon a situation in which he might recommend, with further knowledge, that access should be allowed. It seems proper in such circumstances for the court to intervene to ensure that access does take place during the enquiry and that the welfare officer can report upon it at first hand. A flexible order for supervised access will provide the opportunity for observation and assessment, and will also allow for the situation to be monitored and regulated as the interests of the child may dictate.

The case of Maria and Henry affords a suitable illustration of the use of supervised access for the purpose of assessment.

> Henry and Maria, aged eleven and seven, lived with their father, in whose favour an order for interim custody had been made. Access was in dispute and a welfare officer's report had been ordered. Father maintained that both children resisted the idea of seeing their mother very strongly and were acutely distressed both before and after her sporadic visits to them. Mother, who lived a considerable distance away, contended that the children looked forward to and enjoyed her visits. She suggested that any distress after the event was occasioned by father's effective demand that they should not have enjoyed themselves and by their consequent need to dissimulate in order to remain in his good graces. Henry

maintained that he did not wish to see his mother, but failed to convince the welfare officer that this was his genuine feeling in the matter. Maria, an extroverted and uninhibited little girl, simply agreed cheerfully with whatever happened to be the last suggestion anyone had put to her.

The court, at the welfare officer's suggestion, ordered that the next six full days' access should take place at fortnightly intervals and under his supervision. It also allowed him considerable latitude as to how far the children's wishes should be respected in the event of any serious opposition on their part. A further welfare report was to be filed in three months time, when the future of the access provision would be reviewed.

The welfare officer's task was eased by the mother's suggestion that access during this summer period should take the form of picnics and other outings. She realized the need to overcome the constraints of lengthy meetings in an artificial environment, and was anxious to organize matters so that the children could have the freedom over a long afternoon and evening to relax and to relate to her as normally as possible.

Henry refused to see his mother at all on the first occasion and she accepted the welfare officer's view that he should not be pressed too hard to do so. He continued adamant in his refusal in the weeks that followed, being greatly infleunced by his father's bitter and self-righteous hostility towards his former wife. The starkly contrasting attitudes of the children worried the welfare officer considerably. He concluded, however, that Henry's enforced participation would only serve to destroy his sister's obvious pleasure in the outings and that access should therefore continue with Maria alone.

Maria was highly enthusiastic from the outset and seemed in no way affected by her brother's refusal to participate. From a boisterous and unthinking beginning, in which the prospects of an outing *per se* probably played a greater part in her reckonings than any consideration of the person with whom it was to be, she came to develop a genuine warmth and affection for her mother during these their first regular meetings since the separation. Although still too young to understand why her mother had left, she could now begin to appreciate that she herself was still loved and wanted.

The demands upon the welfare officer during this period were extremely heavy, not only in terms of the time spent with mother and daughter, but also in his role as counsellor to both parents and to the non-participating Henry. The exercise was justified by the fact that he was able to report to the court much more comprehensively and with much greater confidence than he had done on the first occasion. He considered that there should be fortnightly access to Maria on an unsupervised basis and a nominal order for reasonable access to Henry, so that he should not feel permanently excluded or rejected because of his present attitude. An order was made in the terms proposed and a resolution thus obtained in keeping with the needs and interests of both children. This, in the light of the parents' still conflicting accounts of events, would not have been attainable by any other means.

The court also made supervision orders in respect of both children. This provided the welfare officer with a firm base from which to pursue his continuing conciliation work with the parents and with Henry, and also allowed him to monitor the new arrangement for unsupervised access to Maria.

Supervised access can be similarly used in cases where there has been a prolonged separation between the applicant parent and his child. The anxieties of both the custodial parent and the child are wholly understandable in such circumstances, but the viability of the proposed reintroduction of access must remain unproven unless it can be put to some controlled and limited test. The welfare officer's attendance at the initial meetings will not make them any easier for the participants; if anything it will make them even more tense and unnatural. The knowledge, however, that they are under his control and can if necessary be suspended against a formal adjudication by the court can do much to allay anxieties which might otherwise be insupportable. Again the role is a combined one of monitoring and reporting and again, after a suitable series of meetings, the welfare officer should be better placed to advise the court as to whether access should continue.

Supervised Access as a Means of Protecting the Child

More difficult to evaluate, but still within the legitimate confines of supervised access, are those cases in which the custodial parent seeks to deny contact on the grounds that the child might be ill-treated or abducted by the former partner.

The welfare officer here has to assess not only the quality of the relationship between the child and the applicant parent, but also whether the fears of the custodial parent are likely to be realized if access is permitted without supervision.

Protecting the child against ill-treatment

The chances of a child being physically or mentally abused during a period of supervised access are fairly remote. The applicant parent knows that his behaviour is under scrutiny and he is likely to conduct himself with a becoming measure of restraint. The task of actually protecting the child, whilst implicit in the process of supervision, is thus unlikely to exercise the welfare officer very greatly. His principal task is still one of evaluation, but with a specific and concentrated focus. He will be guided in part by the child's willingness or otherwise to see the absent parent. A strong negative reaction, containing obvious elements of fear, will usually speak for itself. He must, however, guard against reading too much into what appears to be a positive response: studies of child abuse cases leave no room for doubt that a well established parent–child bond can withstand a considerable amount of direct physical violence. A friendly and fearless approach to a suspect parent offers no guarantee that all is well.

The problems of assessing whether a parent with an alleged propensity for physical violence will visit it upon his child if access is unsupervised is a most difficult and delicate one. The history of the parent both within the marriage and outside it may offer better guidance in the end than the observed responses of the child. Supervised access may thus contribute relatively little to a positive decision, but it remains an important eliminating process and can contribute actively to a negative one. Needless to say, it is the child and not the parent who should be given the benefit of any continuing doubt.

Protecting the child against removal

There are two main types of case in which the fear is commonly expressed that the child will not be returned to the custodial parent after access. Whilst the danger of abduction will be dramatically diminished in either circumstance by the presence of the welfare officer, supervised access will be seen to offer more possibilities of constructive help in the one case than in the other.

The first group concerns parents of foreign origin. When the parent has established links with and easy access to his homeland the fear of unauthorized removal during access may be considerable. This applies particularly with Asian and African families, where the native culture does not accept that a separated mother should ever have the custody of her children. The sense of shame and disgrace which many fathers feel when they are denied custody in an English court may lead them to attempt to return to their country of origin and to take their children with them. They may give little or no indication of their intention either during the welfare enquiry or during any subsequent period of supervised access which the court may order in an attempt to safeguard the mother's position. Unless this supervision is to be continued on a permanent basis – an arrangement which would finally prove unacceptable to parent, child and welfare officer alike – it is doubtful whether its institution is of any real value: the danger of removal, if it exists at all, will not diminish with the passage of any given number of weeks or months.

Supervised access may serve, on occasion, to confirm that the combination of personality and cultural factors which together create an unyielding commitment to securing possession of the child at any cost would render unsupervised access unsafe. Conclusions of this kind are, however, likely to have been reached in any event at the enquiry stage. A much more characteristic situation is the one in which the welfare officer remains as uncertain of the degree of risk at the end of the period of supervision as he was at the beginning. The court is then left to assess the possible dangers of unsupervised access with little objective evidence to assist in its decision.[1]

The second main group of potential 'snatchers' are the young, immature and sometimes quite seriously disturbed parents whose marriages have failed at a comparatively early stage. They will often remain heavily if unrealistically committed to obtaining possession of their infant children at whatever cost or consequence, where indeed they are capable of considering consequences at all. Their own needs swamp all other considerations, and neither orders of the court nor any objective assessment of the child's needs and interests weigh with them at all. When one act of unlawful removal has taken place, the danger of the child becoming a shuttlecock between the conflicting parents is all too real.

The supervision of access in situations of this kind is clearly essential for the protection of the child. It is also valuable in terms of assessment because it enables the welfare officer to see the parent in what is for him or her the condition of greatest stress, that is, in the physical presence of the child. It is highly charged emotionally and is very demanding on the skills of the welfare officer. Such parents have been known not only to try to remove a child, but also to contemplate causing him serious and deliberate injury when frustrated in the attempt. The parent may reveal by his behaviour, as he could do in no other circumstances, that he is for the present quite unable to cope with only an occasional contact with the child, other than under conditions of strict security. This is not to suggest necessarily that he should be denied contact entirely. A sufficiently skilled welfare officer may over the course of time be able to help him tolerate a restricted amount of access. Supportive counselling may even bring him to the point at which access can be contemplated with a reducing measure of external control.

Supervised Access: Its Proper Use Defined

In the uses of supervised access which have been described, it has been commended as a means of assessing and monitoring the parent–child contact over a specific period of time. The object is to assist the court in arriving at a more permanent decision about the future of the access arrangement, but it is essentially a social work tool made available through a judicial order. As a social work tool its appropriate implementation can only be decided upon by the application of social work values, with which courts are not always fully conversant. From this it follows that it should not be imposed without prior consultation with the welfare officer or without his approval.

As an adjunct to or an extension of the welfare enquiry, the process will probably contain a substantial counselling element. The need for conciliation is implicit in the circumstances which lead to the order being made. Important as the counselling element is, however, it cannot override the reporting function, or release the court from an ultimate decision as to the pattern of access, or its denial, in the future. This is to say that supervised access is not a solution in itself to the problems which make it necessary, and that it cannot therefore be entered into on an indefinite open-ended basis. It can never be more than a means of arriving at a decision as to whether or not access can be permitted to proceed on an unsupervised basis.

Even were the resources of the welfare service such as to be able to contemplate permanent supervised access – and emphatically they are not – the interests of the child would demand that the process be terminated in the end. The benefits to him of a relationship so fraught with difficulty that he could never safely be left with his parent would in the long run be too questionable to justify its continuation. The choice, in the final analysis, must be between unsupervised access and no access at all. The intermediate stage of supervision by a welfare officer can be no more than a temporary expedient, introduced to assist in the determination between these two alternatives.

ACCESS – A VALID PROCESS?

It has already been suggested (see page 54) that welfare officers, involved as they usually are with the problems which access can create, may tend at times to forget that the cases which cause them difficulty are the exception and not the rule. The majority of access situations do proceed happily and undramatically and never call for their intervention. This restatement is important, because whilst the concentration has inevitably been upon its darker aspects, there has throughout been an underlying assumption that where access can be made to work successfully, it is in the child's best interests for it to do so.

There is, however, a current body of opinion which would question seriously the validity of any legally determined provision for access. The desirability of social work intervention to try to 'make' access work would also, by extension, be similarly challenged. Custody, it is held, should be a single, final and irreversible decision, with the decision as to whether access should be granted, and any definition of its terms, being left solely in the hands of the custodial parent.[2] The arguments put forward in support of this view – the child's need for security in his relationship with the custodial parent, his problems in relating to two parents who are in conflict and the potentially devastating effect which such divided loyalties may have upon him – have already been identified as factors which may sometimes justify the suspension or permanent termination of access. They do not, however, appear to be strong enough to justify the conclusion which is drawn from them. It is said with truth that the court can neither make nor break the psychological relationship between the child and his absent parent. What is not taken into account, however, is the capacity of the custodial parent to destroy that relationship, even when it has been much enjoyed and valued by the child. To leave access solely in the gift of that parent, often to be withheld for reasons quite unrelated to the child's welfare, may even serve to disrupt the very relationship which it is seeking to preserve.

The crucial factor which is neglected in this approach and which by contrast is clearly reflected in the most recent adoption legislation,[3] is the deeply felt need of the child who has been separated from a parent to know about his biological origins as well as his psychological parenting. The adopted child is thus allowed access at his majority to relevant information about himself, even though it may be at some considerable emotional cost to his natural parent. If this need is recognized in a child separated from his parent at birth, how much more relevant must it be for the one who has experienced a still-remembered relationship with his absent parent. This relationship, established during his most impressionable early years, may well have contained many positive elements despite the background of marital disharmony. This would seem to be much too important a part of his life to be severed at the casual whim of one parent alone, or even worse, as an act of calculated malice against the absent one.

The advantages to the child of a properly working access relationship are almost limitless, ranging as they do over the whole gamut of influences which go to make up the integrated adult personality. Access can help him to retain a realistic image of the absent parent, rather than a memory distorted by the unhappy experience of the one with whom he lives. It can help him to adjust with less self-doubt and guilt to the fact of his parents' divorce and to understand in his years of maturity, without necessarily seeking to judge, why it was that their marriage failed. This in its turn may help him to avoid internalizing the possibly jaundiced view which his single parent holds of the opposite sex and ultimately repeating the established pattern of marriage failure. It is all too likely, especially in the hurt and anger of the divorce proceedings, that the custodial parent will not be able to see far enough ahead to perceive such potential benefits. This should not be a sufficient reason for a unilateral declaration that access shall not be. In the vast majority of cases, its possibilities at least remain eminently worth exploring.

Good access is beneficial to children, and both the court and its welfare service have their separate parts to play in trying to bring it about. Both have perhaps been guilty of too zealous a pursuit of good access, with a consequent failure to recognize the damaging effects of bad access. What must now be acknowledged with much greater readiness is that access which does not work satisfactorily can be positively harmful to the child, and that it should be abandoned at an earlier rather than a later stage, whilst its ill effects are still retrievable.

5

Reports to the Court

AUTHORITY

The authority of the court to call for a welfare officer's report is to be found in Rule 95(1) of the Matrimonial Causes Rules 1977: 'A judge or registrar is empowered at any time to refer to a court welfare officer for investigation and report any matter in matrimonial proceedings which concerns the welfare of a child.' The authority is thus couched in the widest possible terms. It does not restrict the court to such issues of custody, access or satisfaction as may be before it, but allows for investigation at any stage where it is considered to be warranted.

Neither the parties themselves nor their legal representatives may approach the welfare officer directly to request that he prepare a report. Provision is made, however, under Rule 95(2) for them to invite the registrar to order that a report be made. This distinction is important because it safeguards the impartiality of the welfare officer's position: he is still seen to be reporting on behalf of the court, rather than at the behest of and by implication to the potential advantage of one or other of the parties.

The facility for requesting a welfare officer's report is similarly available to probation officers and other social workers when, from their particular knowledge of a family's situation, they consider that this would be of assistance to the court. Their channel of communication is the divorce court liaison officer, who will then on their behalf request the registrar to order the report.

TYPES OF REFERRAL

Requests for welfare officer's reports will usually fall into one of six main categories: satisfaction, custody, access, pre-decree, injunction/interim custody and wardship.

Circumstances frequently arise in which more than one issue is to be determined by the court and in which the report will be required to satisfy more than one purpose. It therefore follows that there can be no stereotyped format for the various types of report. The notes which follow are intended only to suggest the principal characteristics of each type of referral.

Satisfaction

Section 41(1)(b) of the Matrimonial Causes Act 1973 prohibits the making of a decree absolute unless the court has declared:

> that the only children who are or may be children of the family to whom this section applies are the children named in the order and that –
>
> (i) arrangements for the welfare of every child so named have been made and are satisfactory or are the best that can be devised in the circumstances, or
>
> (ii) it is impractical for the party or parties appearing before the court to make any such arrangements.

Special provision is made [Section 41(1)(c) and 41(2)] to waive the requirement in exceptional circumstances, on the undertaking of the parties to bring the question of arrangements before the court within a specified time, but unless the court has decided that it is not practical to demand it, the general practice is for the decree absolute to be withheld until satisfaction has been declared.

Under the Special Procedure which was introduced in April 1977 for undefended causes, the judge interviews the petitioner in private at a Children's Appointment after the decree nisi has been pronounced. At this appointment, assisted in some courts by a welfare officer, he determines whether or not he can declare himself satisfied with the proposed arrangements. He may also interview the respondent, although the attendance of the latter is not compulsory, even if the children are in his or her care.

The judge may decline to express his satisfaction either because there is specific cause for concern about the children or because there is insufficient evidence upon which to base a decision. This can happen when a petitioner appearing alone has lost touch with his children and has no knowledge of the circumstances in which they are living. The judge then declares that he is 'not satisfied' as to the arrangements made. The terminology is unfortunate, since most parents interpret it as a statement of active dissatisfaction, whereas it is often only a formula for obtaining further information. A welfare officer's report is usually ordered when the certificate of satisfaction is refused, although there is a strong case for requiring parties to provide necessary basic information for themselves rather than delegating the task automatically to the Welfare Service.

The welfare officer's responsibility in referrals for satisfaction is limited to establishing on behalf of the court the adequacy or otherwise of the proposed arrangements and to making any appropriate recommendation as to supervision or, exceptionally, care proceedings. Many judges favour brevity in satisfaction reports, and so long as it is remembered that the enquiry must still be full and thorough, a relatively brief account of a satisfactory situation will normally suffice. Where supervision or care proceedings are recommended it will be necessary for the welfare officer to go into enough detail to justify the course of action which he proposes.

If custody is in dispute at the nisi stage the judge will not usually deal with the question of satisfaction unless it is known that the custody hearing will not take place for some considerable time. In that situation, he may wish to consider the arrangements on the basis of the *de facto* custody position, so that the making of the decree absolute is not unreasonably delayed. More conventionally, however, both issues will be adjourned to a full hearing against the preparation of a welfare officer's report. The referral will be endorsed 'to be directed as to custody' and the report will be required to serve the two-fold purpose. In this, as in the parallel situation in which a serious dispute over access comes to light during the Children's Appointment, the subsequent pattern of enquiry and of reporting will be, if not more searching, at least substantially more complex.

Contested Custody

Custody may be contested at any stage. From the moment the petition is filed to the point where the child passes by reason of age from the jurisdiction of the court, the issue is potentially a live one. Few judges are willing to hear a contested custody application unless a welfare officer's report has been prepared, and in many courts it has become the practice to call for one as soon as it is clear that the parties are indeed in dispute.

The detailed processes of enquiry and of reporting which follow are examined later. It is sufficient at this stage to emphasize that the task of the welfare officer here is to prepare a comparative document in which he will attempt to explore the total situation in each of the proffered environments and to set out in detail their relative advantages and disadvantages.

It is because the task is one of comparison as well as of evaluation that it is essential for the enquiry to be conducted by one officer only, even though the parties may be living in different parts of the country. It is clearly impossible for two separate officers, each reporting on half a situation and able to offer no valid comparisons, to assist the court nearly as effectively as a single officer with first hand knowledge of both sides of the case.

Disputed Access

As with a contest over custody, the court may be called upon to adjudicate in a dispute over access at any stage after the petition is filed. There are further broad similarities with the custody application insofar as a specific issue is in dispute, and the court is unlikely to proceed without a welfare officer's report. Here, too, it is customary in the 'split' situation for a single officer to conduct the whole enquiry.

Disputed access differs from contested custody in that the

parties are asking the court for separate and often incompatible solutions, instead of competing, as it were, for the same prize. The need is for mediation rather than absolute judgment; as the custody report is a comparative document, so the access report is a negotiating one.

Access, as has previously been suggested, is a potentially fertile area for the counselling approach. Where it succeeds, a relatively brief report may be possible, presenting in its conclusion an agreed solution as the basis for a consent order. When conciliation fails, a much more detailed recommendation may be called for and the welfare officer will need to be particularly alive to the possibilities of supervision as a means of resolving the still outstanding difficulties.

It will quickly become apparent in some contested custody cases that there will be a residual problem over access whatever the decision the court reaches. Conciliation in advance of that decision will rarely prove practicable, and the welfare officer will need to direct his enquiry to both issues. The court will then be able to make suitable provision for access at the same time as custody is determined.

Pre-Decree

In some cases the registrar may decide immediately upon the filing of the petition that a welfare officer's report is necessary. This situation arises most commonly where a child is in care or under supervision, or is suffering from a physical or mental disability. It may be, alternatively, that the circumstances of one or both of the parents are such that the court will clearly be unable to express its satisfaction until a full enquiry has been conducted.

In the majority of cases, the pre-decree referral will be in effect an anticipation of the need for a satisfaction report. An apparent conflict over custody or access as demonstrated by the divorce petition and the acknowledgement of service does not justify referral at this stage: in many instances the apparent conflict will have been resolved by the time the matter comes to court. Referrals stemming from genuine applications for interim custody or access before the making of a decree nisi should be treated as fully contested enquiries, to be directed according to the nature of the application.

Injunction/Interim Custody

It is becoming an increasingly regular practice to call for a welfare officer's report in the situation in which a mother combines an application for interim custody with one for an order to restrain her husband from personal violence and/or to expel him from the matrimonial home. As there is no facility either for ordering welfare reports or for determining the custody of the children under the Domestic Violence and Matrimonial Proceedings Act 1976, such applications must still be made as a part of divorce proceedings unless they are made in conjunction with a custody application under the Guardianship of Minors Acts.

In these cases the welfare officer's report must be produced quickly. A holding order or an undertaking from the husband will usually be in force to contain the situation, but the interests of the children will almost certainly demand a swift if not necessarily final resolution. An interim report to help find a solution to the immediate impasse may pave the way to a more considered approach to the long-term problem. The welfare officer will not be called upon to make any formal recommendation as to whether the injunction should be granted or continued, or whether the husband should be excluded from the matrimonial home. He should, however, be in a position to advise the court as to the possible effect upon the children of the adoption of any of the various expedients open to it.

The report will have elements of satisfaction because it will provide information about children in circumstances where they could be at risk. Interim custody may not be contested, although opposition will be more likely if the husband sees in it a means of resisting his proposed expulsion from the home. Access too may prove contentious if his concealed objective is reconciliation and he seeks to use it to maintain contact with his wife. Specific short-term proposals in either case may assist the court considerably in determining the best interim arrangements. Attempts at conciliation are probably better left to the less pressurized atmosphere of the full welfare enquiry which will usually be ordered when the temporary dispositions have been made.

Wardship

Wardship proceedings are brought in the Family Division of the High Court under the Law Reform (Miscellaneous Provisions) Act 1949 and the Guardianship of Minors Acts. In these proceedings the application is to make the child a Ward of Court – in effect, to place it in the custody of the Court. The applicant will usually be seeking to protect the child against a specific hazard, such as unlawful removal from the country or unsuitable or inadequate upbringing by a parent. Proceedings are most often brought either by an aggrieved parent or by another relative. The court determines whether or not wardship shall continue, and if it does, to whom the care and control of the child shall be granted; provision can be made for access and there is the power to make a supervision or a care order.

It is customary for a welfare officer's report to be ordered before any determination is made in such wardship proceedings. From the welfare officer's point of view, the enquiry can be treated in the same way as a contested custody and access case: essentially the same considerations apply to care and control in wardship as they do to custody in divorce proceedings.[1]

THE METHOD OF ENQUIRY

Divorce enquiries involve probation officers with a clientele which covers the entire social spectrum. The only common feature is the stress and anxiety which unite virtually all the parties in proceedings which affect their children; their responses in this highly charged and emotional area are infinitely varied. Each new enquiry demands a genuine flexibility of approach if none of its nuances are to be lost. A retreat into the comparative safety of stereotyped and over-rigid patterns of enquiry, in which welfare officers can be seen on occasion to take refuge, can only be to the detriment of their full appreciation of the situations that they are called upon to assess.

Whilst there can thus be no blueprint for a 'standard' divorce enquiry, there are nonetheless broad areas to which the welfare officer will always be expected to direct his attentions and which do have certain common features. Some possible methods of approach to the problems which can be presented are suggested in the descriptions which follow.

Documentation

The welfare officer's first task is to familiarize himself with the initial information with which he is provided. There are considerable variations in the amount of documentation which divorce registries and liaison officers make available to reporting officers. Some provide little more than a summary of essential information, such as names and addresses of parties and children concerned and the purpose of the referral. Others provide photostat copies of all the relevant documents from the divorce file; these will include the order requesting the welfare officer's report, the divorce petition, the answer (where there is one), the statement of arrangements for the children, details of the application, any affidavits in support of or in opposition to it, and any previous welfare officer's reports.

Whilst a full set of documents can be of much assistance to the welfare officer in planning his enquiry, a note of caution should be sounded about petitions, answers and affidavits. These are by their nature and purpose frankly one-sided documents, and the welfare officer should not automatically accept all that they say at face value. One would hesitate to endorse the old adage that 'truth will emerge even through an affidavit', but it is not without its point. Certainly the contents of such documents should be treated as guides to areas of potential difficulty rather than as unchallengeable truths.

The Parents

The allocation of welfare enquiries is based in principle on the current address of the children concerned. The officer charged with the enquiry will thus always see the custodial parent. In contested issues, as has already been suggested, he will normally see the absent parent as well, whether or not the parties are still living in the same area. The same does not apply in satisfaction and pre-decree referrals where, assuming there are no matters seriously in contention, he can arrange for a distant absent parent to be interviewed on his behalf by a local colleague.

The custodial parent

The custodial parent[2] will need to be seen on several different occasions and preferably in a number of different settings. Meetings should be arranged both at the home and away from it, with the children and without them, and both with and without any second partner there may be. In a straightforward satisfaction enquiry this may be encompassed within a single office interview and two or three home visits. In a contested issue a series of meetings may be necessary both at home and at the office. Joint interviews with both parents can also be helpful, especially when access is in dispute.

The welfare officer's objective will be to assemble as complete a picture as possible of the custodial parent. This will extend beyond the practical and emotional aspects of child care to include functioning as a divorced parent, as a second partner where this is relevant, and in the critical if ill-defined area of home maker in the broadest sense. Although there are many factors involved, and some of them sufficiently intangible to defy detailed description, the task here is still comparatively uncomplicated. The welfare officer has the advantage of seeing parent and children in their natural surroundings and has only to evaluate an actual rather than a largely hypothetical arrangement.

The absent parent

The extent of the welfare officer's involvement with the absent parent will depend to a large extent upon the type of report being prepared. In a satisfaction case where all appears well with the children, it may be restricted to a single interview. It may then amount to little more than advising the absent parent that the report has been ordered and allowing him the opportunity to comment upon the children's situation. The contact may, on the other hand, raise new issues material to the enquiry which the welfare officer will wish to take up with the custodial parent. He may also find it necessary to travel to interview the absent parent himself, if serious difficulties are suggested in the course of an enquiry conducted on his behalf in another area.

In contested issues the welfare officer will have essentially the same objectives as in his work with the custodial parent, but the fact that the children are not living permanently in the home will give rise to a variety of complications. Attempting to assess relationships and parenting capabilities within the artificial confines of observed access is fraught with problems. When access is being denied, or geographical factors make it impossible to see parent and children together, there will be no actual performance at all against which they can be measured. The value of seeking independent confirmation of any opinions that may be formed can hardly be over-stressed.

The practical management of the enquiry will be more difficult if the absent parent lives a long way from his children. Circumstances can change quite radically during a lengthy and complex investigation and a single interview with the absent parent is unlikely to suffice. The welfare officer must therefore be prepared to make more than one journey to the distant home, although he should also remember that some controls can be exercised over this potentially time-consuming aspect of the enquiry. There is no reason why a committed parent should not travel to meet him on occasion and the telephone offers further alternatives when once face-to-face contact has been established.

The Pattern of Enquiry

The fact that a series of meetings will be necessary with both parents, at least in contested cases, points to the need for careful planning in the welfare officer's approach to his enquiry. Every case will develop its own distinctive characteristics as the work progresses, and it would clearly be impossible to prescribe for every eventuality beforehand. The early tasks to be achieved with the parents are nevertheless readily identifiable, as too is the rationale behind the working method proposed.

The initial interview

The primary purpose of the first meeting is to establish a working contract between the parent and the welfare officer. The welfare officer will explain why the report has been ordered and how he plans to go about preparing it. He will explain what it will involve for the parent in terms of time and of intrusion into his personal affairs. He will describe the scope of the other enquiries that he will wish to pursue through schools, doctors and other agencies and will ask permission to put them in hand. He will seek confirmation, and if necessary clarification, of the parent's broad position in relation to the application before the court. This will provide the opportunity to outline his other possible role as conciliator between the parties and to test out the probable response to any overtures in this direction.

For the parent the first meeting will often be used to ventilate his understandable anxieties and possible feelings of resentment over the ordering of the report. Many parents will need to talk about the marriage and its breakdown, often in a self-justifying manner, perhaps in an attempt to present themselves to the welfare officer as the 'good' partner and parent. Some aspects of this unburdening may well be best suited to the privacy of an office setting, beyond all possibility of overhearing by the children.

A further advantage of holding the first meeting at the office is that it allows the parent to concentrate entirely on the matter in hand, away from the inevitable minor distractions which home and family provide. The implied courtesy of a set appointment and the uninterrupted attention of the welfare officer can go far towards establishing an equally committed and positive response in return.

Home visiting

The initial office interview will usually be followed by a visit to the home. This is in many ways the most crucial setting in the whole enquiry. It is here that the welfare officer will first meet the children and any other members of the household. Here too he will consider the pattern of relationships within the home and the general level of functioning of the family unit. Ultimately he will have to try to assess the quality of life which this environment can offer to the children.

While doubtless largely preoccupied with intangible factors of this kind, he will also take into account the material provision made for the children. He will want to ensure, for example, that they are adequately housed, clothed and fed, and that there are suitable arrangements for their care during parental absences. Contested issues will rarely hinge upon such matters, but he still has a duty to be satisfied that basic needs are being properly met.

Visits to the home, in the early stages at least, should be made by appointment. The parent should be encouraged to prepare himself for the meeting by marshalling in advance the ideas and arguments he will wish to put forward; the welfare officer, after all, will have done no less. The pre-arranged visit can also help to prevent misconceptions such as that the welfare officer's primary function is to check without warning upon standards of child care, or even to try to catch the parent out in some irregularity in his private life. The consideration it implies for often hard-pressed lone parents can also help to foster a sound working relationship.

This is not to suggest that there is no place for unheralded visits. They are obviously essential where there are suspicions that children are being left unattended or otherwise neglected. They can also be revealing where the welfare officer considers that children are being over-prepared for their meetings with him. They should, however, be left until the later stages of the enquiry, unless the safety of the children calls for more immediate action.

The continuing contact

With the working contract set and the principle of home and office meetings established, each case will begin to make its own individual demands, and preconceived ideas as to the most suitable pattern of contact will cease to be helpful. Even the balance between home and office interviews will be determined by the needs of the separate parties and the demands of the enquiry as a whole.

The welfare officer will proceed from the established contract to the gathering of information for his report. The rate at which people can work at this varies considerably, and not necessarily in accordance with the complexity of the material or the intensity of the emotions generated. The implications of the information obtained must next be shared with the parents, and again there is no uniform rate of assimilation. Some will need much more help than others in understanding and accepting the welfare officer's interpretation of the emerging situation. Finally there is the question of conciliation, and here the time span in quite incalculable. Lengthy extensions of the enquiry process can be fully justified if a consent order appears to be attainable.

If the pattern and time scale of the enquiry cannot be fully determined in advance, the frequency and regularity of the welfare officer's contacts with the parties can. There should be no substantial gaps between meetings and certainly no unexplained ones. The enquiry period is bound to be stressful for the parents, and uncertainty as to when the next meeting will be, and for what purpose, adds needlessly to their anxieties. Joint planning as to the timing and content of interviews will at least provide the security of a known framework of operation.

Second Partners

The second relationship

Second partners are of critical importance when custody and access are contested, whether or not the new relationship has been formalized by marriage. The welfare officer's first concern will be with the nature of the relationship itself. Some second partnerships are contracted as a considered judgment, others as a 'rebound' response to a recently broken marriage. Some are prompted by loneliness, a flagging self-esteem or a simple inability to cope alone, whilst motives of affection and of personal fulfilment figure largely in others. Some new partners will have learnt much from their previous experience, others will be repeating an earlier pattern of failure. The welfare officer will use some of these yardsticks in assessing the quality of the relationship and attempting to judge its present stability and its prospects of enduring.

The previous experience of the new partner both in the marital relationship and in the rearing of children will need to be explored. Some will already be husbands or wives and they may or may not bring children of their own to the new family unit. For others it will be a new type of relationship, perhaps bringing them into close contact with children for the first time.

The partner of the custodial parent

The functioning of the second partner of the custodial parent will be assessed as a part of the welfare officer's consideration of the total home environment. His task will again be the easier because he will be dealing with a situation which is already in being. If the relationship is of recent origin he will be properly cautious as to the conclusions he can reach, but he will be able to observe at first hand how both adults and children appear to be adapting to it.

When the new partner brings children of his own to the reconstituted family unit, a further dimension is added to an already delicate balance of relationships. The interaction of the two sets of children and their responses to both natural and surrogate parent are of obvious importance. Equally significant are the attitudes of the adults to both their own and their partner's children, with the complementary dangers of undue attention on the one hand and possible scapegoating on the other. The welfare officer will want to be sure not only of the parents' appreciation of the various hazards of their new *menage,* but also of their capacity for adjustment should it be called for.

The role in which the second partner casts himself or is cast in relation to the children is of major significance. When the new partner is a woman, and particularly when the children are very young, many of the practical functions of motherhood, such as feeding, clothing and general daily care, will often be effectively thrust upon her. How far she attempts to undertake the emotional aspects of mothering will depend on how she and the father interpret her role. They may decide for the sake of the children's emotional security that she should mother them in the fullest sense. Alternatively, and this may well apply if access is prospering, they may wish to distinguish between her caring and still loving function and an area of true emotional dependence which is to be the province of the natural mother alone. The welfare officer will look for confirmation that she is comfortable in the chosen role and that it is acceptable to the absent parent. Confusion or anxiety in the children, uncertainty in the surrogate, or serious dissatisfaction on the part of the natural mother may suggest the need for some realignment.

The role of the second partner as father-substitute seems open to wider extremes of interpretation. Some men accept little or no emotional involvement with the children, seeing themselves exclusively in the role of provider and leaving virtually every aspect of parenting to their mother. Others take to themselves a full parental role, to the extent of seeing the absent father as a rival not only for the children's affections, but for those of his former wife as well. Access inevitably provides a ready focus for this kind of defensive hostility, and conflict in the face of its attempted denial is not uncommon.

Disagreement between the mother and her second partner over his role seems to be more frequent than when their situations are reversed. The children are more likely to be confused as to the parts which he and their natural father should play in their lives, and their prospects of finding lasting security under his regime can suffer accordingly. Here, as with the potential access problem, the welfare officer's task will be as much one of counselling as of evaluation.

The partner of the absent parent

The potential of an absent parent's partner as a surrogate mother or father is clearly of great importance, but it will in practice prove most difficult to assess. The opportunities for first-hand observation will be fewer and less reliable and, although the welfare officer may seek to apply the same criteria as for the other parties principally concerned, he will rarely arrive at equally firm and satisfactory conclusions.

If the new partner has custody of his or her own children the welfare officer will be able to form some opinion as to parenting capacity. He will not, however, be able to assume that the same standards of care would be extended automatically to other children. The new partner may not be able to cope with additional children on a permanent or even a temporary basis, and the threat which they could represent to the stability of the existing family unit may well be feared or resented.

When the second partner is a parent who does not have custody, the prospect of becoming a surrogate parent to someone else's children can provoke very mixed reactions. At times, the children will be welcomed as a substitute for the absent family, with a potential for future difficulty which scarcely requires elaboration. At others, feelings of loss and of deprivation will be heightened to the point where they can hardly be accepted at all. The position is further complicated when an understandable but mistaken sense of loyalty to the applicant parent discourages the new partner from voicing quite strongly felt reservations.

The second partner who has no children and no real experience of them presents a fresh set of problems for the welfare officer, who may be left with little more than good intentions to report upon. Prolonged staying access can help, but only up to a point. It may, for example, enable him to make negative judgments about a custody application with reasonable safety, but it is too artificial an arrangement upon which to base any strongly positive recommendations. The conclusion that such a partner would in all probability cope successfully with the demands of full time parenthood is one the welfare officer will rarely be able to reach.

The Children

There are no circumstances in which it is not necessary for the welfare officer to see children who are the subjects of a welfare enquiry. He must still see personally children who are in the long-term care of the local authority (see page 108) and infants and even babes in arms, with whom communication is manifestly impossible.

In the latter instance, although the welfare officer may feel the need for a more expert opinion as to the prevailing standards of baby care, he should still be able to draw some conclusions as to both attitudes and capabilities by simple observation of parent and child together.

Interviewing the children

The children, like their parents, should be seen in as many different situations as can be arranged. They should be seen with the parent with whom they are living, and a meeting in their own home with that parent will provide a convenient introduction. They should also be observed in the company of the second partner, if there is one. The welfare officer will also need to see them both individually and collectively, without any other adult present. A similar pattern of contacts should be set up in the home of the absent parent, subject always to the constraints of what may be a limited access facility, and any practical problems of time and distance.

The welfare officer's concentration will again be mainly upon the less tangible aspects of the situation. The children's relationships within the existing family unit and with the absent parent and his family will be a major focus. The welfare officer's concern should be seen to range beyond the immediate issue of custody, access or satisfaction, and to embrace the child as a complete personality in his own right. A demonstrated interest in home, school, friends and all the outside enthusiasms of the moment will not only assist in the building up of a working relationship, but will also provide the perspective through which the quality of the total environment can be examined.

The pattern and duration of the ongoing contact with children is no more easy to anticipate than with their parents. Some will relate much more readily to the welfare officer than others, and there will be wide and unpredictable variations both in their willingness to reveal deeply-felt emotions and in their verbal skills when they do try to express them. Some will be under much greater pressure from their parents than others, perhaps affecting their sense of security to a degree which will make their trust and confidence immeasurably more difficult to gain.

The strength of a parent's influence over a child should never be under-estimated: to see a child in a different room from a dominating mother or father may well not be to see him alone. The whole of the home environment can be so redolent of the parental personality as to inhibit completely his capacity for independent thought and expression. The welfare officer can seek to overcome this problem in a variety of ways. For the older child, provided he is not overawed by the more formal atmosphere, an office interview may be helpful, especially if he is of an age to make the journey unaccompanied. There is the added advantage that he can see from this individual attention that his personal investment in the proceedings is being properly recognized. With younger children a walk in the park or a ride in the welfare officer's car might provide the avenue to a more natural and spontaneous communication.

The welfare officer must take care that his pursuit of the children's confidence does not result in a backlash of suspicion and antagonism from the parents. This danger can at least be minimized by keeping the parents informed not only of what it is proposed to do, but why; by inviting cooperation rather than seeking to impose an imperfectly explained method of enquiry.

Explaining the enquiry

Unless the child is too young to understand or it is considered inadvisable in the face of parental opposition to inform him, the welfare officer should explain, in terms appropriate to his age and understanding, why the enquiry is being conducted. This need not be done at the first meeting, or at least not other than by way of a very generalized introduction, since it is preferable to establish some kind of *rapport* with the child before moving into potentially sensitive areas. In the case of the younger child this will present few problems, since he will usually accept with little question the occasional and unexplained appearance of a strange adult within his orbit. He would in any event probably be overwhelmed and subsequently inhibited by too full and formal an explanation in the beginning stages. Explanations should not be too long delayed with older children, who may become puzzled and anxious if they are left for too long in doubt as to the welfare officer's specific purpose. Here too, however, it must be remembered that too swift and concentrated a focus upon the material issue may discourage later discussion of the more apparently mundane facets of the child's daily living, which are also important to the welfare officer's overall appraisal of his situation. The aim should be to establish a measure of mutual confidence before explaining in detail what the enquiry entails, but that confidence can itself be eroded if the child feels that it is being sought to no definite purpose.

Over-elaborate explanations should always be avoided. The child who wants more detailed information will make this clear; it is better to offer little, and gradually expand at need, rather than to impose more than the child is ready to accept. The concept of a satisfaction enquiry is usually uncomplicated and unthreatening, and explanations here will rarely present problems. More finesse is needed in the approach to contested issues, about which children can become acutely anxious. The level at which the explanation is pitched will be determined not only by the child's age and intelligence but also by his understanding of the application before the court. At the most simple level, the welfare officer may find that he needs to describe his role only in terms of helping the court and the parents decide what it is best to do. To older, more intelligent or more sophisticated children, his exposition may need to be as comprehensive as that which was offered to their parents.

The welfare officer should avoid presenting the situation explicitly as one of conflict between the parents, with the implied burden upon the child to choose between them. Rather, he should encourage the child to look upon him as an ally who is trying to help everybody involved to arrive at a solution to the problem. He must take care in so doing not to allow the child to invest him with powers of ultimate decision which he does not possess. He will be aware that some parents do create in their children the impression that the welfare officer is virtually omnipotent in determining their future, and he must be ready to correct this misapprehension. A proper explanation both of the limitations and of the potentially helpful aspects of his role will often induce a more relaxed and more constructive response on the child's part. This process of explanation and clarification with the child is in many ways similar to the original setting of the working contract with the parents.

Establishing their views

The decision whether or not to discuss a contested issue directly with the child concerned and, either implicitly or explicitly, to invite him to express his opinions about it cannot be reduced to any simple rule of thumb. Age must clearly be a factor, and some children will be excluded from this aspect of enquiry for this reason alone. There are, however, other considerations such as intelligence, maturity and emotional security. These factors too will guide both the welfare officer and the court in deciding how much weight to attach to any preferences which may be expressed. This is, however, very much an area of blurred and indistinct boundaries, and over-simplification can cause unnecessary and distressing pressures for children of whom too much is being asked and too directly.

Techniques of indirect evaluation can be helpful with small children. The interpretation of play and of written material is a specialist field into which the welfare officer should not perhaps venture too far without appropriate support, but it can undoubtedly be most illuminating at times. Alternatively, he may choose the more simple expedient of considering with the child the things he would most wish for in an imaginary world. This will often allow the child to convey those hopes and fears that he is unwilling or unable to put into words in the context of his real-life situation.

When more than one child is the subject of an application the children should all be seen separately by the welfare officer as well as in a group. This will guard against the danger of a dominant child acting as spokesman for a whole family and submerging the wishes and feelings of its individual members beneath his own strongly-felt opinions. It will also allow the child who is not at one with his brothers and sisters to give expression to his own doubts and anxieties without the fear that what he says will be reported back to a possibly angry parent.

In the full discussion of custody and access issues, much stress was laid upon the power of parental pressure and upon the feelings of responsibility, anxiety and guilt which it can generate. The welfare officer must take care not to add to the child's burden by appearing to ask him to choose between the conflicting demands of his parents. His views may be invited, in due recognition of the fact that he is the person most directly affected by the proceedings, and that as such he has the right to be heard should he so wish. He should not, however, be forced into the position in which he feels compelled to state a preference and neither, in the event of his doing so, should he be permitted to assume that this will be the determining factor in the court's adjudication. Many a child will feel that he has been relieved of an intolerable burden when it is made clear to him that the responsibility for the final decision does not rest with him alone.

Other Relatives

The welfare officer will sometimes find himself under pressure from one of the parties to interview a number of relatives or family friends in the course of his enquiries. The difficulty with many such interviews is that the people whom he is invited to hear are much too partisan in their approach. He could indeed be forgiven for thinking on occasion that they are more concerned to promote the family's cause than the children's welfare. The value of such enquiries cannot, however, be dismissed out of hand: some relatives will display a surprising capacity for objective observation and offer a contribution which is of genuine assistance to the enquiry.

Unless he receives specific directions from the judge or registrar, the welfare officer has complete discretion as to his chosen areas of enquiry. It is for him to determine whether or not interviews with members of the extended family would be likely to assist him. He may find it helpful in reaching his decision to establish how well the relative concerned knows the children and how significant a part he or she has played in their upbringing. A grandmother who assists a working parent by looking after children outside school hours and during holidays may well have pertinent observations to make about them. Another relative, on the other hand, may have very strong views about the rights and wrongs of the marital situation, from which quite false inferences have been drawn about custody or access. He may have little direct knowledge of the children and none at all of the criticized partner as a parent.

Feelings can run high in extended family enquiries and the welfare officer must ensure that he is not improperly influenced by the sheer intensity of the emotions aroused. Neither, on the other hand, must he fail to sift through what may be a welter of irrelevant material for any information which does have a direct bearing upon the children's welfare. The issue of their welfare is always his principal concern and any direct evidence on this score must always be considered. Any information which is produced about the parties' behaviour within the marriage will not concern him unless it casts doubt upon their ability and suitability as parents.

The Local Authority

The welfare officer will find in some cases that the children upon whom he is required to report are in the care of the local authority or subject to its supervision. In many pre-decree referrals this will indeed be the reason why the report has been ordered.

Where the local authority involvement is a substantial one, some courts are content for the social services department to prepare the report in its entirety, at least in uncontested issues. A strict interpretation of the relevant rules[3] throws some doubt upon the practice, since they make it clear that the designated welfare officer must be a probation officer and do not make any provision for him to delegate his responsibilities to another agency. The correct procedure therefore is for the welfare officer himself to report in all cases. He will, of course, invite the local authority to report upon its involvement with the family, but he should still conduct a sufficient enquiry to be able to verify the information that is provided. The social worker's report will normally be much the more substantial and more helpful document, but in theory at least, it can only have the status of a supplement to the welfare officer's contribution.

This is a needlessly cumbersome procedure. It requires an undesirable duplication of work and it is seen by social services departments, not without some justification, as a slight upon their abilities to report adequately upon their own clients. The system is not without its incidental advantages: there is merit, for example, in an independent report when a child is in care and the local authority has been instrumental in bringing that situation about. On balance, however, it seems preferable by far that the social services department should have sole responsibility for reporting in those uncontested cases in which it is currently involved.

Other Agencies

Besides seeing the children and the adults most directly concerned in the matter before the court and consulting where appropriate with the local authority, the welfare officer will need to make enquiries of a number of other agencies who may have knowledge of the family. These enquiries may relate either to the children or to the parents. The parents should always be informed of the proposed enquiries and of the reason for them, and the findings should be discussed with them. Their consent should be obtained wherever possible, but the welfare officer can, in the final analysis, pursue whatever lines of enquiry he considers to be necessary, even if consent is withheld. Enquiries of this kind must be made in every case, whether the referral is for satisfaction or whether it relates to a contested issue.

No comprehensive check list can be drawn up of all the possible lines of enquiry, but the following notes do describe some of the most common and most useful areas of consultation.

Schools

If a child is of school age his school should be visited by prior arrangement. His performance should be discussed with the headteacher and, if possible, with the current class teacher. The need to visit the school is emphasized; the off-the-cuff responses on the telephone of a busy headteacher, who in some cases may have only a limited knowledge of the child concerned, are not sufficient for this type of enquiry.

The main concentration should be upon the child's social functioning, with special attention being paid to any signs of emotional disturbance or insecurity. Academic ability is of no particular significance in itself, but performance in relation to potential, whether up to or appreciably below it, may be revealing.

School visits are of particular value in the case of infant and junior school children, who frequently tell their teachers much of what is going on at home and how they feel about it. These spontaneous comments, made away from all possibility of parental pressure, have a validity entirely their own. The drawings that a child produces and the odd illuminating comment in his written work can also be quite powerful indicators of his feelings about his situation.

Schools can also be helpful in evaluating the effect that

access is having on a child. This is particularly useful where the parental accounts conflict. A child may voice his views directly to his teacher or, more commonly, he may indicate by his behaviour both before and after the access period how much he is enjoying the contact and how well or badly he is coping with the pressures which it may entail.

Day nurseries and play groups

A visit to the day nursery or play group of a pre-school child will serve much the same purpose as a school visit in the case of his older brother or sister. The impartial comments of the trained outside observer will nearly always add an extra dimension to the welfare officer's own perceptions.

The staff of the day nursery or play group will usually have observed sufficient of the parent's handling of the child to be able to offer pertinent comment. They will often know how well the parent is managing in his or her given circumstances and may also have views as to the basic standard of care which is being provided. Attitudes in matters such as access are also on occasion expressed with far greater frankness in this setting than is considered expedient in the welfare officer's presence.

The medical profession

The general practitioner should be visited if there has been recent or regular consultation in respect of either the children or their parents. This applies whether the consultation has been for formal physical or psychiatric illness or for more generalized nervous or emotional problems. Many doctors are unwilling to provide any information without the written consent of the patient and this it is well worth while to obtain in advance.

The doctor can be invited to comment upon the physical health of the children and the standard of physical care which they are receiving. If he is aware of any emotional difficulties he may be asked for an opinion as to their likely cause. Enquiries can likewise be made as to the physical and emotional health of the parents and, where there is or has been illness, comment may be invited as to its potential or actual repercussions in terms of that parent's ability to care adequately for the children.

The welfare officer should clarify with the doctor which of his comments may be discussed with the parents and which of them will find a place in the final report. The doctor should be offered the option of furnishing a written report, which he may find preferable to being quoted in an overall context over which he will have no final control. The practice of including a written report is a sound one, but the welfare officer may later find himself in difficulty if a fee is requested. Neither the court itself nor the Welfare Service is empowered to make payment. It is the responsibility of the welfare officer to establish whether a fee is being asked for, and to arrange between the parties, their solicitors and the doctor how and by whom it will be paid.

If a child or a relevant adult has had recent hospital treatment the welfare officer should arrange either to see the consultant personally or to obtain a report from him. The same broad areas should be covered as in an enquiry to a general practitioner and the caveats with regard to written consents, unauthorized quotation, and the payment of fees apply if anything with even greater force.

Health visitors

Health visitors are a valuable source of information about all pre-school children and especially about infants. Many welfare officers are much assisted by an opinion more professional than their own as to the standard of care which babies are receiving. The health visitor is in a unique position by virtue of her continuing involvement to offer an opinion not only as to whether a very young child is thriving as he should, but also as to the mother's ability to care adequately for him. This can be a crucial contribution and it should never be overlooked.

Other social work agencies

It is not uncommon for the welfare officer to discover in the course of his enquiries that another social work agency such as the NSPCC or the Child Guidance Service is actively working with the family or has recently been doing so. In this situation he should meet with the social worker concerned to discuss the family's circumstances in the light of the proceedings before the court. It is customary to invite the outside agency to prepare a report giving details of its involvement and its assessment of the family's position. This report is submitted by the welfare officer as a supplement to his own.

The Probation and After-Care Service

Where the Service is itself already involved by virtue of a statutory responsibility or voluntary commitment in respect of parents, children or second partners, the question arises as to whether the supervising officer should himself conduct the welfare enquiry. The proposition is at first sight an attractive one because of the knowledge which he already possesses, and it may on occasion also be a feasible one, provided that the parties and their legal representatives are content with it. In many cases, however, the person under supervision will feel himself to be disadvantaged if his probation officer is used in this way. There is certainly much to be said for the separation of the civil and criminal responsibilities of the Service and for the avoidance in principle of this kind of overlapping.

The Service cannot always afford the seeming luxury of such an automatic separation, and the best practical solution is for the divorce court liaison officer to consult with the supervising officer and his senior as to the feasibility and desirability of his conducting the enquiry in any given situation. If it is proposed provisionally for the two functions to be combined, the views of the parties should be ascertained at the outset; any objection to this combination should be respected. Where separation of the reporting and supervising functions is decided upon, it is incumbent upon the nominated welfare officer to confer with the supervising officer in the same way as he would with a social worker from another agency.

The Police

In spite of the acknowledged reluctance of the police to involve themselves in domestic issues, the welfare officer might reasonably expect their assistance to the extent of establishing or confirming the criminal records of the parties whose circumstances he is called upon to investigate. Home Office regulations as presently interpreted make this impossible. The position is anomalous in that criminal records can be made available to probation officers preparing social enquiry reports in criminal proceedings and to local authority social workers making enquiries with a view to fostering. Both these categories are included in the prescribed list of situations in which disclosure is permitted; enquiries for the divorce court are not and it is held that there is no discretionary power to extend it.

The dangers of this situation are self-evident. The welfare officer may in ignorance recommend that a parent or second partner with convictions for offences against children remain in immediate proximity to further potential victims. The court, in equal ignorance, may endorse that recommendation. It is essential that information of this kind should be available to the court and the welfare officer has a clear duty to include in his report details of any relevant convictions which may be known to him. The present arrangement whereby he can only obtain such information from his own departmental records or through the direct admission of the parties concerned is manifestly unsatisfactory. The need for a fresh directive in this matter is urgent.

THE WELFARE OFFICER'S REPORT

The findings of the welfare officer on the completion of his enquiries are, other than in exceptional circumstances, presented to the court in the form of a written report. A judge may occasionally ask for an oral report after a very brief adjournment – perhaps as little as 24 hours – when he is faced with the need to decide upon an appropriate interim order in an emergency. The seizure of a child by an absent parent who alleges his safety to be at hazard is a typical example. It is not intended to base any final order on the welfare officer's preliminary findings. The objective is only to ensure that the child's welfare is properly safeguarded while a full enquiry is conducted and a conventional written report prepared.

Format of Report

There is no generally accepted format for the welfare report, but some practices are common to most areas. Basic particulars such as the names and addresses of the parties and the names, ages and whereabouts of the children are normally presented either at the beginning of the report or on a separate front sheet.

This is frequently followed by a statement of all the people who have been interviewed or contacted by the welfare officer in the course of the enquiry. The need for such a statement is questionable, provided that the welfare officer's sources of information are made explicit in the main body of his report, with any opinions other than his own being appropriately attributed.

A brief summary of the events leading to the ordering of the report provides a useful general introduction. Some officers, possibly confused as to its purpose, provide at this stage a detailed history of the marriage, which is not good practice. The object is to provide the reader with sufficient information to place the application before the court in an easily digestible context. It should therefore include the following information: a simple formal statement about the marriage breakdown – who left whom, and when, and what happened then to the children; a chronological account of any previous adjudications concerning either the marriage or the children; any significant changes in the circumstances of the parties or their children since the separation; brief details of the current issue before the court and of when and by whom the report was ordered. This section should contain only objective statements of fact: the expression of opinions about the events described is not appropriate.

In considering a suitable format for the main body of the report it should be remembered that it is essentially a working document. It will be referred to in detail by judge and counsel, and it should be broken down into numbered and headed sections for ease of reference. An unbroken narrative style is not desirable. Separate sections should relate to the principal protagonists: petitioner, petitioner's wife, respondent, children, etc. A separate section relating to access is often helpful. The report should end with a summary of the main features of the case which may but need not necessarily include a formal recommendation as to disposal (see page 117).

Content of the Report

The fact that reports in satisfaction cases and in contested issues are prepared for different purposes is reflected both in their content and their length.

Reports for satisfaction

A satisfaction report is intended only to enable the judge to reach a conclusion as to whether suitable arrangements have been made for the welfare of the children concerned. It is essentially a descriptive document, which should contain basic information as to the circumstances in which the children and the custodial parent are living. It is also evaluative in that the welfare officer is required to assess whether he considers that the provision made is adequate at both a material and an emotional level.

The report should contain a brief description of the physical environment and some account of the personality and capabilities of the custodial parent; a similar account of the personalities and activities of the children and of their apparent state of physical and emotional well-being; the views upon the situation of any other relevant agency and also those of the absent parent; and the welfare officer's summing up of the family's total circumstances.

As previously suggested, there is no need for a lengthy report where all is found to be well. It is only in less satisfactory situations, where the welfare officer will need to substantiate a recommendation for supervision or for care proceedings, that a detailed account of the situation is called for.

Reports in contested issues

The purpose of the enquiry, which is to assist the court in reaching a decision that is in the best interests of the children, provides the best guide for the welfare officer as to what information he should include in his report. This applies particularly to the adult principals in the case: everything which is included about them should be relevant to this central issue. Their personalities, temperaments and parenting abilities will obviously be material; so too will be their relationships with each other and with the children and the circumstances in which they are living. Their behaviour within the marriage will not be relevant unless it bears directly upon the children; a long and detailed history of events prior to the breakdown will not therefore be appropriate. There is indeed positive danger in dwelling at excessive length upon the marriage itself. The welfare officer who, whether directly or by implication, begins to attribute guilt for the breakdown may find it difficult to prevent conclusions in this area from prejudicing his consideration of the parties in their parental roles.

The children should each be dealt with separately in the report. There should be brief pen portraits as to personality, intelligence and disposition, and it is useful to comment upon the overall impact of the parental separation where this can be gauged. Relevant medical history should be recorded but, as with the parents, excessive detail should be avoided unless it impinges directly upon the court's decision. Reports from schools, as from the medical profession or any other agency, should be specifically attributed. The welfare officer should state whether he has discussed the application with the children. He should summarize any views they express and indicate, if he can, how derivative or how spontaneous they are and how strongly they are held.

Where access is a live issue it is best considered in a separate section of the report. The existing arrangement should be set out, with a statement as to whether this is a voluntary or a formally defined provision. The areas of agreement and of dissent should be outlined, together with each parent's proposals for the future. The views of the children should also be commented upon. The welfare officer should attempt to evaluate the proposals of the parents in terms of their likely impact on the children, and should formally state his findings. If the proposals of neither parent in his view fully meet the children's needs, he is at liberty to suggest a suitable alternative arrangement.

Anxiety is sometimes expressed by less experienced welfare officers about the length of reports in contested matters. It is in fact rarely possible to encompass a proper consideration of all the issues in a complex family situation in other than a quite substantial document. Provision is made for both judge and counsel to consider the report at comparative leisure before the hearing, and provided that the content is relevant and the presentation clear and concise, length need not in itself give any cause for concern.

Recommendations

There are two distinct types of recommendation which it is open to the welfare officer to make at the conclusion of his report. The first relates to the way in which the court should deal with the issue of custody or access which is before it, the second to the making of supervision orders or the institution of care proceedings.

Recommendations as to adjudication

Welfare officers were not originally encouraged to offer advice in the determination of contested issues. This view has gradually lost favour, and it is now generally held that a reporting officer reaching a firm conclusion as to where the best interests of the children lie should make his opinion known to the court. Provided that he sets out clearly the reasoning behind that conclusion, and is able if necessary to support his argument verbally at the hearing, most judges will now welcome his formal recommendation.

The pendulum seems indeed to have swung too far on occasion, with some judges expecting the welfare officer always to make a formal recommendation and feeling perhaps less than well served when he fails to do so. This is undesirable. The welfare officer should not be put under pressure to make a recommendation when he feels that the issue is too finely balanced for him to be able to do so. Should he feel that the children's interests would be equally well served whatever the court's decision, this is a conclusion he can legitimately reach. He should then limit his observations to a recapitulation of the relevant factors for and against the application and offer no opinion as to their comparative merits.

Recommendations as to supervision

Section 44(1) of the Matrimonial Causes Act 1973 allows for a child to be placed under supervision where 'exceptional circumstances' make such a course desirable. This term is not defined, and recommendations as to supervision are normally based on the principle of the child's best interests. Those interests may demand supervision even though, in the context of families broken by divorce, the circumstances are in no way exceptional. They will in many cases be only too depressingly familiar.

In practice, the court will not require the welfare officer who recommends supervision to demonstrate that the circumstances are exceptional. It will most commonly be content to accept his professional judgment as to the need and make the order he suggests.

Section 44(1) allows further for supervision to be exercised either by a welfare officer or by a local authority. The welfare officer should make clear in his report which agency he proposes should supervise. He should establish before nominating the local authority that it is willing to supervise. Its agreement should then be recorded as a part of his recommendation. The criteria for choosing the supervising agency are considered in chapter 6.

It should be noted that a supervision order can only be made under Section 44(1) 'as respects any period during which the child is . . . committed to the custody of any person'. The welfare officer must therefore ensure that a formal custody order is made if he is recommending supervision. A supervision order cannot be made in conjunction with a declaration of satisfaction only, which does not of itself confer custody on either party.

Recommendations as to care proceedings

Section 43(1) of the Act empowers the court to commit a child to the care of the local authority. The Rules[4] require, however, that the registrar shall provide the local authority with 14 days' notice of the hearing so that it may make its representations to the court in respect of the proposed order. From this it is clear that the power to make a care order in divorce proceedings does not cater for the emergency situation where a child is at immediate risk. Rather it offers a possible solution to the intractable long-term problem where committal to care may be desirable although the child is in no present and serious danger.

Where emergency action is required, the local authority can still proceed in the conventional way by means of a place of safety order or care and protection proceedings before a juvenile court. The juvenile court cannot make a final order where the divorce court has jurisdiction without the consent of the divorce court judge. Application for this is made through the divorce court liaison officer after the juvenile court has contained the immediate crisis by means of an interim care order. The judge will then usually give his permission for that court to make whatever final order it thinks fit. This practice cannot, however, be followed where wardship proceedings have been initiated. The originating summons in this case has the effect of making the child a Ward forthwith and jurisdiction thereafter is vested exclusively in the High Court. Any subsequent proceedings relating to the child must be heard before a Judge of the Family Division.

When the welfare officer is satisfied that care proceedings are appropriate he should confer with the social services department and ascertain its views in the matter. The authority's readiness or otherwise to endorse his recommendation should be indicated in his report.

Circumstances may occasionally arise in which the making of a care order in divorce proceedings is desirable, but expedition is still necessary in the interests of the child. This can occur, for example, when there are fears as to the possible parental reaction during the period between the serving of the notice and the hearing, but there is insufficient evidence to meet the more exacting proofs required in the juvenile court. Given the consent of the court, the local authority and the parties, the period of notice can be abbreviated or completely waived. It must, however, be stressed that this is an unconventional expedient and is not to be commended as a general practice.

Inspection of the Report

Contested issues

The completed welfare officer's report is filed by the divorce court liaison officer at the divorce registry. The parties' legal representatives, or the parties themselves if they are appearing in person, are then informed by the registrar that the report is available for inspection. A copy of it can be obtained on payment to the registrar of the appropriate fee. The welfare officer must work on the assumption that his report will be read by the parties, whether as a result of their own initiative in obtaining it or in the course of discussion with their solicitors. This is not to suggest that he should pull his punches in the statement of either fact or opinion. The main issues, and certainly any formal recommendation, should already have been discussed with the parties; they may also have been shown the report in draft form, a practice which has much to commend it. It does mean, however, that the welfare officer should take care in choosing how to express himself. He may have to say things which will be hurtful however they are put, but even very severe criticism can be made more acceptable if the welfare officer demonstrates a sympathetic understanding and indeed a measure of compassion for those whose circumstances he is called upon to discuss.

Satisfaction

Satisfaction reports are likewise filed by the liaison officer at the registry. They are then passed directly to the judge who considers them in private. These reports are not normally made available to the parties or their solicitors, although the judge can, at his discretion, order that they should be released. This may happen if a consent custody order is being proposed or if supervision or care proceedings are being considered. The same caveats therefore apply with regard to the making of unnecessarily demeaning or damaging comments about the parties, but the same need for total honesty still obtains.

Releasing the report

The report when filed becomes the property of the court and as such it is not the welfare officer's to release on his own initiative. Parties or solicitors who apply directly to him for a copy should be advised of this position and referred to the registrar.

It is accepted that where a child is made the subject of a

supervision order to the local authority or is committed to its care, the authority should be furnished with a copy of the welfare officer's report. If a social work agency requests a copy under any other circumstances, the matter should be referred to the court for directions.

Retention of the report

The parties to a contested issue, whether legally represented or appearing in person, do have the right to inspect or to bespeak a copy of the welfare officer's report.[5] They do thus have the right to retain a copy of it permanently and herein lies a source of potential difficulty. The parties will often focus upon those passages which appear unfavourable to them and, by brooding upon them out of context, get the balance of the report quite out of perspective. They may also use the report unwisely or improperly, by broadcasting its contents in an inappropriate manner.

It would seem preferable for represented parties to be permitted only to read the report in the presence of their solicitors for the purpose of giving instructions. For the party who appears in person, and who must clearly be provided with a copy, it might be possible to redraft the Rules in such a way as to safeguard the confidentiality of the information to which he has thus been given access.

6

Matrimonial Supervision Orders

LEGAL ASPECTS

The Present Provision

Legal authority
The power to provide for the supervision of children in divorce proceedings is conferred by Section 44 of the Matrimonial Causes Act 1973.

Section 44(1) limits its application to cases 'where there are exceptional circumstances making it desirable that the child should be under the supervision of an independent person' and where 'the child . . . is committed to the custody of any person'. This section also allows for supervision to be exercised by a probation officer or by the local authority.[1]

Section 44(5) gives the court power to discharge or to vary the supervision order. There is, however, only one effective variation in practice, which is to transfer the responsibility for supervision from one of the two nominated agencies to the other.

Duration of the order
The Act does not set any limit on the duration of the order, which can remain in force until the child reaches the age of 18 years. The vast majority of orders are made without specific time limit, presumably in the expectation that supervising officers will apply for them to be discharged when they have served their purpose.

It is clear from the wording of Section 44(1), which empowers the court to order supervision 'as respects any period during which the child . . . is committed to the custody of any person', that restrictions can be imposed as to the length of the order. This is a power which is seldom exercised but which could usefully be invoked with much greater frequency. It is evident in many cases that the need for supervision is likely to be short lived, and the focus of both supervisor and parents could be sharpened by the knowledge that the time available to them is limited. The supervising officer would be able to apply for an extension of the order if a longer involvement proved necessary.

Requirements of supervision

The Act lays down no specific requirements which must be met whilst a supervision order is in force. It imposes no obligations upon parent or child or upon the supervising officer. The order itself will usually require the custodial parent to inform the supervising officer of any change in the child's address, but the authority for even this limited restriction is questionable. Neither in Statute nor in Rule is there any instruction for the supervising officer as to the discharge of his duty or any minimal response demanded of the parent or the child.

Powers of Supervising Officer

Limitations to authority

The supervision exercised under an order made in divorce proceedings is unlike any other form of statutory supervision for which a probation officer can be responsible. The order, as we have seen, imposes no obligations either on the child, who is its nominal subject, or the parent who has charge of him. It cannot therefore carry any direct sanctions. The supervising officer has to operate in an unstructured framework, without the specific controls which are available to him in his dealings with his other clients. He has no power to regulate the frequency or the pattern of his contacts with the family. He cannot direct that the custodial parent or the child should visit him at his office or that he should be received into their home. He cannot insist on seeing the child alone. He may indeed wonder whether he can insist on seeing the child at all!

If the custodial parent, in contravention of the terms of the order, changes his address without informing the supervising officer, there is no immediate remedy which he can seek. The court must of course be informed, but it has no power to issue a warrant for the arrest of child or parent. Various courses of action will be open as and when contact is re-established: custody can be varied or care proceedings instituted. First, however, the child must be found. The supervising officer, having reported the facts to the court, can do nothing further.

When a child under supervision is found to be at immediate and serious risk, the supervising officer has no power to take emergency action. The requirement that notice of intended care proceedings should be served on the local authority[2] makes the only available procedure too slow and cumbersome to be relevant. The local authority has to be invited to seek a place of safety order or to institute care, protection or control proceedings before a juvenile court, just as if no supervision order existed at all. Action may, in the event, prove more difficult to obtain in these circumstances, should the local authority prove reluctant to initiate proceedings because the child is already the subject of a supervision order to another agency.

The supervising officer may perhaps be forgiven for wondering at this point whether he possesses any effective powers at all. There are in fact two courses which he can adopt, should the process of supervision not be developing to his satisfaction. By the first, he can seek the court's directions as to how he should carry out his supervisory duties. By the second, he can institute his own proceedings for the variation of the existing custody order, and such variation can include the committal of the child to the care of the local authority.

Seeking directions

Under Rule 93(4) of the Matrimonial Causes Rules 1977 the supervising officer may apply 'for directions as to the exercise of (his) powers under the order'.

This Rule offers the only effective action short of care proceedings which is open to a supervising officer faced with a parent whose cooperation is consistently withheld. It also offers a further avenue of possible assistance when the parent's attitude over access is not consistent with the best interests of the child. The judge, if he thinks it necessary, can order a further hearing at which he can indicate to the parent the areas in which he expects a change in attitude or performance. In the final analysis, however, his only sanction is to vary custody or to commit the child to care and this, despite the parent's lack of cooperation, would in many cases be quite inappropriate.

The powers available under this Rule are thus in some respects more apparent than real. They make it possible for a difficult situation to be formally and officially ventilated, but this ventilation may only demonstrate that no satisfactory solution is available. In the face of the continued intransigence of an otherwise capable and caring parent, both court and supervising officer may need seriously to consider the desirability of discharging the order as unworkable.

Summons to vary

Rule 92(3) permits a supervising officer to apply by summons, without obtaining leave to intervene in the cause, for an order relating to the custody or education of a child or for an order committing him to the care of the local authority.

The supervising officer will most commonly seek to exercise this power in circumstances where he has concluded that the child's long term interests would be best served by committal to care, although there is no immediate crisis such as would justify emergency action. Such a conclusion is unlikely to be reached without close liaison with the local authority and the joint planning of a suitable programme for the child's future care.

It may occasionally happen that the supervising officer will himself wish to apply for a variation of custody in favour of a grandparent or other relative. This may be for the purpose of ratifying an existing arrangement which is seen to be in the child's best interests and which the welfare officer wishes to place on a secure and permanent footing. Situations do arise in which such an alternative custodian lacks the means to start proceedings himself but is ineligible for assistance under the legal aid system.

An application by the supervising officer to vary custody between the parents is rarely appropriate. When such a variation is necessary in the child's interests, the absent parent will usually be only too willing to make the application himself. Should he not be prepared to do so, the court may legitimately doubt the real depth of his commitment to the proposal.

Discharge of Supervision

The supervising officer may apply at any stage for the discharge of the order. He may do so because he has achieved his objectives in supervision or because he has come to recognize that they are unattainable. This latter consideration is an important one, since persistent attempts to work with a wholly intractable problem, as in some cases of access refusal, can in the end do more harm than good. It may be less damaging simply to abandon a situation which is not amenable to casework help.

The authority to apply for discharge, like that to apply for directions, is contained in Rule 93(4). The application, if unlikely to be opposed, can be made in the form of a letter to the court. 'Any interested party,' which in practice means both parents, has to be notified – if this is practicable. Many judges require both parents to signify their consent in writing before the order is discharged. Whether or not the judge makes this a formal requirement, the supervising officer should indicate the attitudes of the parents in his letter of application. This letter should be channelled through the divorce court liaison officer.

Supervising officers tend on the whole to be over-cautious in their approach to the question of discharge. They are perhaps overawed by the nominal length of the order – 13 years or more in the case of a pre-school child – and are reluctant to accept that its purpose may have been fully and satisfactorily achieved in a matter of months, or at most a year or two. There is, too, a form of inertia which can set in with long-standing orders where there has been a succession of supervising officers. Supervision continues, as it were, almost by tradition, with its original purposes lost. In this, as in other forms of supervision, there should be clear and well-defined objectives; if the supervising officer is no longer certain what he is hoping to achieve, the exercise is in all probability valueless. The nettle should then be grasped and an application for discharge made.

This is not to suggest that there is no case for long running orders. Supervision may continue appropriately for two, three or five years, or even longer. There is, however, an imperative need for regular review in such cases. The supervising officer must always be looking forward towards the possibility of discharge, rather than continuing mechanically to supervise simply because the order is still there.

CRITERIA FOR RECOMMENDING SUPERVISION

Before recommending that a child be placed under supervision the reporting officer must satisfy himself both that there is cause for concern about the child's welfare and that the difficulties which he has identified are potentially amenable to the kind of help it can offer. The welfare officer's concern may relate to physical or emotional factors or, since they can be both interdependent and overlapping, to a combination of the two. In many cases anxieties about the child's welfare will be a reflection of unsolved problems on the part of the parent or parents. These problems and those of the child will often stem directly from the marriage breakdown – presenting difficulties over access offer a classic example – but this will not always be the case. Supervision may offer a legitimate avenue for the exploration of problems which affect the child's well-being but which are of quite independent origin.

Physical Factors

The first responsibility of the welfare officer is to ensure that the child is adequately cared for in a material sense and that he is not at physical risk. Standards in material provision are relative but there are still minimum requirements which can be set in terms of feeding, clothing and general daily care. The attainment of these may have more to do with fundamental parental competence and the will to survive than with purely financial considerations. Absolute standards in terms of avoidance of physical risk are sometimes laid down with more confidence, but here too some allowance must be made for cultural norms. Practices which are seen as quite unacceptable in one social setting may in another have been regarded as satisfactory both by the parents prior to their separation and by the social agencies with whom they were then in contact.

The standard of care which children receive after separation is to a greater or lesser extent dependent upon the ability of the custodial parent to manage in the aftermath of marital breakdown. Some are able to cope admirably, while others fail to do so to the extent that no proper provision is made for their children's basic practical needs. There is no single explanation for this failure to manage. It is possible, for example, to differentiate between the mother whose domestic performance might be described as inherently inadequate, and the one whose former capacity to function satisfactorily has been impaired by marriage failure. The lack of familiarity of some lone fathers with basic domestic routines can expose small children to the risk of physical neglect. Other fathers may be capable of a good standard of parenting, but be unable to demonstrate it in the period after separation. Finally, one must consider environmental factors such as poor housing and social isolation. These may in themselves be a principal cause of inadequate caring or they may serve to exacerbate an already unsatisfactory situation.

The inadequate mother

The inadequate mother, for reasons of extreme youth, chronic ill-health, poor intelligence or ignorance of the first principles of child care, will never have been able to provide her children with an acceptable level of physical care. Her limitations are not a consequence of her marital failure, although it may have served to expose them more completely. She may, up to this point, have slipped through the welfare net and struggled on alone, or she may have received the support and guidance of a battery of social work agencies. Such mothers present the greatest problems when their children are still infants, because it is then that the risks to them are most acute. Assuming that the situation is not so grave as to warrant the removal of the children, the welfare officer must decide whether supervision might ameliorate the difficulties.

If no social worker is currently monitoring the family's situation the decision in favour of supervision may be a relatively straightforward one.[3] Matters can become more complicated when another agency is already on the scene. On the one hand it may be desirable to reinforce its endeavours with the support of a statutory order, which will ensure the court's continued oversight and accessibility. On the other, it may be held that the existing safeguards are sufficient and that the duplication of social work effort will do little to ease the mother's problems.

When other agencies are interested in the family it is always good practice for the welfare officer to call a case conference. This will not only ensure that he has access to all the available information, but will also give him the benefit of other professional opinions in deciding if supervision is appropriate.

In this, as in all cases where supervision is being actively considered, the views of the mother should be sought and her capacity and willingness to respond to it assessed.

The underfunctioning mother

The underfunctioning mother is one who has previously demonstrated good standards of child care, but whose emotional reaction to separation or whose loss of confidence in the face of it has been such as to impair for the time being her ability to manage her family.

In the early stages of separation some measure of depression and loss of self-confidence, and a consequent degree of underfunctioning, are not uncommon. Supervision will not, however, be necessary in every case. Many such mothers are able to work through this phase unaided and indeed prefer to do so, whilst for others there are sufficient in-built supports in the form of friends and family to carry them through until equilibrium is regained. The children, although not as thoughtfully cared for as during the marriage, are still catered for at a more or less acceptable level and are at no identifiable physical risk. Supervision in this situation may be better avoided, since it may further undermine the mother's confidence and prolong her period of adjustment to her single state.

Supervision will be indicated if the period of underfunctioning is unduly prolonged and the management of the children has become so desultory as to drift towards open neglect. This pattern often occurs when the mother is living in a state of social isolation. The absence of any current social work involvement is a common feature. As with the genuinely inadequate mother, the younger the children the greater the need for oversight and guidance will be. The supervisor's objectives here, however, will be less educative and more directed towards self-understanding. It need be neither a long-term nor a very intensive process. He will seek to restore her self-image as a woman and as a mother so that she is able to resume an effective parenting role.

The custodial father

It is probably true today that more fathers than ever before are capable of running a home single-handedly and of cooking and cleaning for, clothing and generally managing even small children on a permanent basis. There are nevertheless still many marriages in which the traditional division of male and female roles is firmly maintained and when these fail, custodial fathers can find themselves at a loss. Initially at least, they may stand in need not only of general guidance, but of basic instruction in discharging their new responsibilities.

Most custodial fathers continue to work and some of them are less sensitive than most lone mothers to the potential dangers to their children of a lack of adequate oversight during holidays and out of school hours. They tend, too, to be less aware of the various sources of assistance which are available to them and they can in consequence suffer needless difficulty. A short period of supervision can often help them to organize the mechanics of single-parent family living so as to eliminate some of the potential risks to their children and to enhance the general quality of their material care.

Doubts are often expressed as to the propriety of lone

fathers caring for their daughters and especially for their adolescent daughters. Their situation tends to be viewed exclusively in sexual terms, with the spectre of incest looming as it were under every bed. There is seldom similar speculation about lone mothers and their sons. It is true, however, that the more intimate aspects of emergent female sexuality can present problems for even the most emancipated fathers. Supervision is not necessarily appropriate, but it can be helpful where a girl is obviously in need of a close and reliable confidante.

Environment

Adverse environmental factors can contribute significantly to a parent's inability to cope with the pressures inherent in managing a family after separation or divorce. They may in themselves be almost overwhelming, or they may be seen more as an additional burden, reducing a limited functioning capacity still further. In either event, supervision can provide the impetus to move forward.

It is now generally accepted that the occupation of the matrimonial home should in principle be the prerogative of the custodial parent. This does not, however, solve the problem of keeping up rent or mortgage payments on what will often be an appreciably reduced income. In the midst of the emotional trauma of divorce many parents are unequal to negotiating with the building society and the DHSS for a new mortgage arrangement or to pursuing the various concessions and benefits which are available in respect of their rentals. Intervention may also be necessary with local housing authorities to dispose of deeply worrying rent arrears for which a newly-separated parent may not be responsible. Lone parents often suffer much stress and anxiety because of doubts as to their right or financial ability to continue to raise their families in the matrimonial home. Assistance through a statutory order can help to make their situation more secure.

Similar help can also be appropriate where the custodial parent wishes to leave the matrimonial home. This may be because there are too many unhappy memories for parent or children to remain contentedly in it, or because the threatened return of a previously violent partner makes any lasting sense of security impossible. A fresh home in such circumstances can mean a fresh start psychologically for the new family unit, but the parent may be unable to achieve it without help.

The welfare enquiry will sometimes take place a substantial time after the marriage breakdown, and the custodial parent may have begun to accept some deterioration in the family's circumstances as inevitable. Living conditions may already be quite inadequate and the will to remedy the deficiency either fading or completely lost. Short-term intervention under the mantle of a supervision order may provide the incentive to the parent and the necessary pressure on the housing authority to put matters right.

The problems of custodial fathers in employment are generally recognized because of their widely accepted role as the primary source of family income. The problems of lone mothers, accentuated by their generally lower status in the field of employment, receive perhaps less sympathy than they deserve. For both there are two possible and complementary problems: that of needing psychologically to work but being prevented from doing so by the demands of a young family; and that of feeling impelled to do so against their better judgment because of the meagreness of state financial benefits or the unreliability of maintenance payments.[4] Mothers and fathers alike can suffer an acute sense of frustration and uncertainty as they attempt to work out their priorities, and the difficulties can be reflected in a very direct way in their attempts at family management. Counselling can be of great value and supervision offers a readily available vehicle for it.

Parents caring alone for their children after divorce need the support and understanding of their friends and families and of the community at large. Most of all they need to be accepted as parents who are not 'different' and not somehow to be blamed for their situation. Social attitudes will tend towards stigmatization rather than acceptance and the common friends of the marriage too often vanish after its collapse. When family and personal friends are far distant, the custodial parent can feel a devasting sense of isolation which can intensify and prolong the natural period of underfunctioning. Lack of confidence can lead to a downward spiral of self-denigration which can in its turn effectively inhibit all powers of family management.

Supervision here can offer much, not only in terms of rebuilding a realistic self-image, but also of providing introductions to suitable clubs and societies. A change of home, the search for a job or membership of one of the self-help groups may all have a part to play, but the genuinely isolated and ego-damaged parent will not venture spontaneously into such undertakings.

Emotional Factors

Incomplete or inappropriate adjustments to separation or divorce, whether by the child, his parents or their new partners, can result in difficulties in his attitudes and relationships both in the present and in the long-term future. Supervision should always be considered in such situations. The child may be more or less involved in the process, according to his age and the sophistication of his perceptions. Substantial work will, however, always be needed with at least one of the parents if adult attitudes and influences are to be modified to his advantage. Supervision in these circumstances is more threatening for the parents and more demanding for the worker than when the problems are of a purely practical kind. It is also likely to last much longer.

The principal criterion in deciding for or against a recommendation for supervision must, as always, be the welfare of the child. The welfare officer should not propose supervision solely on the grounds of what he perceives to be an inappropriate parental adjustment, provided that he is satisfied it is having no adverse effect upon the child. Such adjustments are part of the necessary defensive mechanisms of the separated parent and they cannot be challenged without causing him anxiety and distress. They should not be disturbed unless they are operating at the child's expense.

The specific factors which most commonly lead to a recommendation in favour of supervision are not readily categorized and the boundaries will inevitably be more blurred than in any formal presentation. They are here divided into relationships within the home, transmitted attitudes to marriage and the opposite sex, images of and attitudes towards the absent parent, and access. A measure of overlapping in any given case is assumed.

Relationships within the home

Most children have some ambivalent feelings when their parents separate. The custodial parent is bound to be seen to some extent as having rejected the absent one and any second partner as having supplanted him. The direct ventilation of such feelings, or the indirect expression of them in behavioural terms, may make for temporary or long-lasting difficulties in the child's relationships with the adult members of the new family unit. Parental understanding of the problem and confidence to handle it will sometimes be so limited as to aggravate rather than ameliorate the difficulties. The ensuing tensions can do lasting damage to the integrated functioning of the family.

When parents remain in a state of conflict after divorce it is common for the child to become the focus of their continuing hostilities. His perception of what is happening may be limited, but his awareness will probably be sufficient for him to feel some resentment at the way in which he is being used. This resentment will often be acted out directly in his behaviour.

Tensions between the custodial parent and the second partner will bear particularly heavily upon the child when he himself appears to be the cause of them. Disagreement as to the role of the second partner or difficulties on his part in accepting its inevitable limitations will cause uncertainty and confusion in the child's responses. He may, of course, refuse to accept the second partner in his designated role, even if the parents are agreed about it.

All these aspects of potentially dislocated relationships within the home revolve around the child's ability to find a secure and acceptable position in the revised family circumstances. His failure to find such a position will often point to the need for casework intervention to help both him and his parents.

Transmitted attitudes

The custodial parent exercises the biggest single influence in moulding the child's future attitudes towards the opposite sex in general and towards marriage in particular. Some do convey the impression, despite their own marriage failure, that relationships with the opposite sex are desirable and enjoyable, and that most adults do enter into matrimony with an expectation of happiness and fulfilment which will ultimately be achieved. Attitudes of this kind contribute very positively to the child's emotional development and enhance his prospects of emerging relatively unscathed from his parents' misfortunes.

The embittered lone parent, on the other hand, who needs both to cling to the child and to continue to punish the absent parent, may transmit much less healthy messages. All men may be caricatured as violent, sexually demanding drunkards or all women as brainless, promiscuous slatterns and these stereotypes can be pressed upon the child with an overwhelming intensity. The distorted values will often be further reinforced by the denial of access, a recurrent feature in such cases, and by the conscious avoidance of adults of the opposite sex. The child's psycho-sexual development will be grossly hampered and, if and when he finally rebels against the stifling parental shackles, he will find himself without any model upon which to base his own behaviour and expectations. Herein lie the seeds of the cycle of repeated marriage failure from generation to generation.

Parents of this type will usually show their hand fairly clearly at the enquiry stage and when, as is often the case, they are people of powerful and dominating personality, the danger signals will be evident. Supervision is unlikely to make any immediate impact upon such entrenched attitudes and it may in the end fail to modify them at all. The child, however, will at the least be exposed through it to a more balanced adult outlook and he may as a result begin to re-think his values on more independent lines.

The absent parent

The importance of the absent parent in the child's life extends far beyond such access meetings as may take place.

Except when the separation took place in early infancy, the child will retain some memories of him and will have been influenced in some measure by his personality and presence. This may be admitted freely, or it may be tacitly accepted that the matter is not one for open discussion, but either way the absent parent remains as a very real presence in the new family unit. This applies equally whether or not access is taking place, and denial of this basic fact only adds to its potency. It is for this reason that second partners so often experience difficulty in establishing their separate and independent roles within newly constituted families.

If it is impossible to deny that the absent parent will occupy some place in his child's thoughts and emotions, it is important that the image of him that is retained should be a realistic one. There are dangers in presenting too black a picture, but over-idealization can also bring its problems. When there is no contact and no discussion within the home, the child may well build up a fantasy image which is too perfect to serve as any practical model; he may, alternatively, create one which is without any redeeming features at all. Even when access is taking place, the parental desire to please combined with the child's appreciation of the power which is his to wield can create a wholly unreal situation.

The task of presenting a realistic image of the absent parent, like that of sustaining the access arrangement, falls principally to the custodial parent. It is of critical importance to the child's emotional development that such a realistic image should be maintained, and where it is clear that the custodial parent is reluctant or is genuinely unable to offer this, supervision should be seriously considered.

Access

It is often difficult for the welfare officer to complete his task of conciliation in disputed access cases within the limited time span of a conventional divorce enquiry. The child's welfare will not have been secured if access has neither been satisfactorily established nor abandoned as unworkable, but his interests may demand a hearing before the issue is thus far resolved. With no agreement between the parents, or at best only a temporary accommodation, counselling may be continued through a supervision order. Initial parental opposition to the idea of supervision may be strong, but resistance will rarely be so powerful as to preclude it without a trial.

CHOICE OF SUPERVISING AGENCY

Three main influences contribute to the choice of supervising agency. First, there may be an inter-departmental agreement between the Probation and After-Care Service and the local Social Services Department. Second, where there is no specific policy, casework considerations may point conclusively to one agency or the other. Third, the matter may be determined by local judicial preference.

Inter-Departmental Policy

Age limit

In some areas there is an agreed policy that, other than in exceptional circumstances, the Probation and After-Care Service will not be involved in the supervision of any children below a given minimum age. This minimum age varies from area to area and the principle is not always universally applied. Matrimonial supervision orders do in fact constitute the most common exception, with some probation areas accepting a liability which they would not be prepared to meet in respect of other children of similar age.

Current involvement

It is generally accepted that where either department has an existing responsibility in the family, that department shall exercise supervision. Both conservation of resources and the dictates of good casework practice require that this should be so.

Previous involvement

When an agency's involvement with a family has only recently been terminated, and especially when the former supervising officer is available to offer continuity, the case should be treated as effectively current.

Practice varies when the agency activity has been less recent. It will depend partly upon the rigidity with which the age limit principle applies and partly upon the local image of each department as the 'natural' supervising agency. When the issue is genuinely in doubt, it should be decided upon the basis of which agency can, in functional terms, better provide the particular kind of supervision that is called for in the case in question.

Casework Considerations

Probation and After-Care Service
The Probation and After-Care Service is usually the more appropriate agency when the object of supervision is to continue with conciliation work which has already been started during the welfare enquiry. The reporting officer will be certain both of his social work objectives and of how best they might be attained. It is obviously to the client's advantage if continuity can be maintained. This will not always be possible: the specialist welfare officer could in the course of time become so inundated with supervision orders made at his own suggestion that he would become unable to discharge his primary duty of preparing reports.

Even where continuity is not possible, it is still preferable for a probation officer to supervise. In the present state of development of the two agencies, probation staff are usually better attuned to the ethos of divorce court practice and better able to handle the intricacies of, say, a continuing and contentious access problem. Local authority social workers are as yet less well equipped by training or experience to undertake this type of supervision, and it is questionable in some of the more hard-pressed urban areas whether they are able to afford a high enough priority for such non-crisis work.

Social services departments
Supervision by the local authority would seem in general to be more desirable when the issue involved is specifically one of child care rather than of post-marital conciliation. The resources of social services departments are better geared than those of the Probation and After-Care Service to dealing with the problems of caring for very young children, and they are at times more adept at mobilizing suitable social

work and other supports for the inadequate parent. They have an overall responsibility for and a wider experience of children at risk, and action required in respect of these situations may be more smoothly initiated when they are the supervising agency.

Judicial Practice

Where the welfare officer's report indicates which agency it is thought should supervise, this is accepted by many judges without discussion. If there is no recommendation on this point, the decision seems to be based either on accepted local practice or on the subjective preferences of the individual judge between the two services. Some judges, certainly, do seek to differentiate according to the needs of the case, but the practice is not very widespread and the decision is governed too often by the simple accident of geography rather than by anything else.

This is an area where there appear to be no clear guidelines and one to which insufficient attention has perhaps been paid. Not all judges appreciate the different styles of supervision that can result from their orders, or that one agency may be better equipped to handle a particular type of case. It might perhaps be of help if they were to indicate both what they hope supervision will achieve and why it is being entrusted to the agency which they are nominating.

SUPERVISION IN PRACTICE

Many of the practical issues of matrimonial supervision are implicit in the suggested criteria which have already been discussed. Other facets will have become apparent earlier in the chapters on conciliation, reports to the court and access. The areas which remain to be considered in detail are the focus of supervision, the place of the child in the process and the problems peculiar to this area of work.

The Focus of Supervision

Matrimonial supervision presents particular problems of focus. In the first place, the work may not be directly with the child, although he is the nominal subject of the order. The emphasis will often be upon the attitudes of the adults who surround him. The custodial and absent parent and any second partners are all crucial in determining his well-being, and any conciliation which can be achieved between them will be to his advantage.

The marriage itself, although now legally dead, may continue to present problems for child and parents alike, and the circumstances of its failure may require particular attention. In some cases work will be needed with all the principal parties virtually simultaneously.

There is, in the second place, always some risk with an order of indeterminate length that supervision will not be sufficiently incisive. This is particularly true where there is the potential for a very protracted involvement, and successive supervising officers may muddle on at times in an almost random fashion. The lesson is obvious for matrimonial supervision, where there are a number of different areas demanding attention. Work must be carefully planned, with specific short-term and long-term objectives, and its progress must be systematically reviewed. The supervising officer is then aware of why he focuses on a particular area at any given time, of how this activity fits into the overall pattern of his handling of the case, and of what impact it may be expected to have upon the situation as a whole.

The marriage breakdown

All matrimonial supervision orders are a consequence of marital breakdown. This fact may seem too self-evident to need stating, but it is one nonetheless which a surprising number of supervising officers manage to ignore. This is most often the case when they have not themselves conducted the welfare enquiry or when, as will still occasionally happen, the order is made without benefit of a welfare report.[5] The kind of supervision which results from this neglect tends to deal only with presenting problems on an *ad hoc* basis, or is restricted to a monitoring of the child's physical well-being. Extended over a substantial period of time this can be a somewhat arid process, and it can indeed degenerate into a more or less meaningless exercise.

The marriage breakdown suggests itself as an early focus for supervision because, apart from the fact that it is the one common denominator in every case, it is the lynch pin upon which the attitudes and behaviour of the parties are hinged. The time span of the welfare enquiry will rarely have allowed for a sufficient investigation of its intricacies and it is doubtful in any event whether this is the most appropriate setting for the undertaking. The parties' main concern at the enquiry stage is properly with the present contest over custody or access. They may appreciate that the history of the marriage and its breakdown has a bearing upon the attitudes which have led to the disputed court case, but it is not a matter they will wish to consider in detail while the main issue remains unsettled. The more leisurely and comparatively tension-free framework of supervision will usually offer a more suitable setting for this kind of long-term work.

It is not proposed that supervision should always entail a detailed dissection of every facet of the failed marriage. To embark upon such a programme could well be to dismantle to no good purpose the defences which the parents have established. The marriage breakdown is relevant only insofar as the attitudes and behaviour to which it has given rise may threaten the emotional well-being of the child.

Parental attitudes and behaviour cannot, however, be examined in a vacuum. To be understood they must be seen against the background of the marriage as a whole, its good qualities as well as its bad, and the reasons, in the parents' estimation, for its failure. The supervising officer must obtain this general picture of the marriage if he is to appreciate the present problems. He must, however, be selective in deciding which aspects of it require his further attention, and his activities should be controlled by the overriding consideration of how best they can contribute to the child's welfare.

The absent parent

The role of the absent parent in the child's life has already been seen to be of critical importance. It is generally recognized as a legitimate focus for supervision when access is taking place, and particularly when it is presenting problems. Less attention tends to be paid to the absent parent when all is going smoothly, although it is in fact still desirable for contact to be maintained with him. The fact that access presents no active difficulties does not mean that he, his child and his former partner are automatically free from problems in their relationship with each other, and the opportunity to deal with them in an atmosphere of relative calm and cooperation should not be ignored. There is too the added advantage that it is easier, in the event of an unexpected crisis, to work from the basis of a relationship of established confidence rather than to approach the difficulty cold with a comparative stranger.

Supervising officers tend most often to exclude the absent parent from their calculations when access is not taking place and there has been no recent contact between him and his child. This is unfortunate, because it is precisely in this situation that the unresolved difficulties of divorce are most likely to be found. Here, above all, conciliation will be necessary. This approach is especially unrealistic when the supervising officer colludes in a conspiracy of silence about the absent parent. He still remains a figure of major significance to the child and the custodial parent, and failure to acknowledge this fact can only be to ignore a most important aspect of their lives. Even in situations where any resumption of access cannot be envisaged as the remotest contingency, the need for a bridge between the absent parent and his child still remains. At the least, he can be kept informed of the child's progress and development, and the child and his custodial parent helped to face up to the fact of his continued existence. He can be presented then as a living personality with ordinary human hopes and feelings, and above all as a person with whom some present communion is being maintained.

Conciliation

Some attempt at conciliation is implicit in every supervision order which is made as a result of emotional rather than purely physical or environmental problems. It is taken conventionally to be a service which is offered to the divorced parents, but it can have equal relevance for their children. The form which the counselling takes will vary considerably from case to case, but the objective of modifying the total emotional environment for the benefit of the children will be constant. The process will of necessity be a long term one and it will permeate every aspect of the supervising officer's involvement.

The concept of conciliation can thus be described as an expression of the ethos of matrimonial supervision rather than as a separately distinguishable task within it. The focus is therefore an imprecise and ill-defined one. This does not mean that the supervising officer cannot or should not identify the various intermediate goals through which he seeks to achieve the ultimate conciliation. It is indeed essential for him to do so if he is to engage in constructive work with his clients rather than simply to entertain well-intentioned hopes of future good will between them which are too amorphous to be attainable. The aspects of planning and of review are perhaps more important here than anywhere, not only because this long-term objective of supervision is incapable of precise advance definition, but also because it is the one upon which the success or failure of the whole enterprise will finally be seen to rest.

The Place of the Child in Supervision

The extent to which the child is actively involved in the process of supervision will depend upon a number of factors. The reasons for the making of the order will be relevant, as too will his age, intelligence and the level of sophistication at which he appreciates the issues involved. Access will be a typical sphere in which the level of his contribution towards the resolution of existing problems may vary considerably. But whether he participates very fully or only to a limited extent, or whether he does not do so at all, the fact that he is under supervision will involve the agency in certain fundamental responsibilities towards him.

The duty of the supervising officer

Unless specifically relieved of it by the court, the supervising officer has a basic responsibility for oversight of the child's general welfare at both a physical and an emotional level. From this it follows that he has a duty to see the child regularly. The fact that the child may be too young to take any active part, or that it is his parents rather than he who are the principal focus of the casework activity, does not in any way lessen that responsibility.

The supervising officer will be very much aware of the responsibility in cases of possible ill-treatment or neglect and in those cases where a custodial parent is clearly underfunctioning. It may well assume a lesser significance in situations where the physical provision for infant children is not suspect and the task is essentially one of conciliation between their parents. The purpose of seeing custodial parent and child together in such circumstances will usually extend far beyond a simple monitoring of standards of physical care, but this will always remain a relevant consideration.

The practice has evolved in some courts, where supervision would not have been contemplated but for the potential recurrence of access problems, to endorse the order 'limited to access'. The effect of this is to relieve the supervising officer of his customary duty to maintain some oversight of the child's welfare as a whole. It is accepted that he will exercise no conventional supervisory function, but will only become involved at the invitation of either parent, in the event of renewed difficulties over access.

This formally sanctioned arrangement to supervise only when necessary does seem to provide parents with an added sense of security, whilst removing in their eyes the implied stigma of a full supervision order. They do appear to treat it as a more helpful resource than the alternative of seeking assistance on a purely voluntary basis and it can thus help to ensure that only the genuinely intractable problems are referred back to the court. From the supervisor's point of view, it provides the added security of knowing that he has the court's approval to remain inactive when supervision would be serving no useful purpose.

Indirect supervision

This term is used to describe those situations in which, although the child is the nominal subject of the order and although, as we have seen, he will still have some contact with the supervising officer, he will take little or no active part in the proceedings. The cases in which this type of supervision is appropriate fall into four broad categories.

The first is that of infant children, who are too young to have any appreciation of the fact of their parents' separation. Since they are also below the age at which they can communicate their ideas and feelings to other people, they obviously cannot contribute to supervision in any active sense.

Observation of the interaction between the infant child and his parent can nonetheless be of considerable assistance to the supervising officer in assessing the overall health of his emotional environment. The way in which the custodial parent handles him, and the ease or otherwise with which his physical needs are met, can be an effective barometer of the parent's wider social functioning. Tension, impatience and inconsistency all offer their own warning signals, whilst confidence, calmness and demonstrated contentment in the parental role can equally provide some measure of reassurance.

This observation can also provide the springboard for unselfconscious consideration of other issues affecting the child. The physical activity of tending him may distract some attention from the immediate impact of the spoken word. It may also evoke memories and feelings about the absent parent's former role with the child; consideration of his present and future role may then come more easily and naturally than in a more formal and intellectualized setting. This is an excellent example of the multi-faceted character of the home visit. The physical and emotional well-being of both child and parent are unobtrusively monitored, whilst the occasion is provided for a reasonably comfortable discussion about less tangible but potentially more disturbing matters.

The second category concerns cases in which the main objective of supervision is to improve the child's physical environment. He will have little direct part to play, regardless of his age, since supervision is only undertaken to help his parent to obtain better housing, appropriate financial assistance or relief from the problems of social isolation. The child will benefit from the supervising officer's intervention, but the work is essentially adult-orientated, and it is from the custodial parent that the response is being sought. It may well be appropriate, if he is old enough, to keep the child informed of what is being done and why it is necessary, but nothing will actually be asked of him.

The third category is that of the underfunctioning or inadequate mother of young children, who will often be unable to create or to sustain an atmosphere in the home that is conducive to their proper emotional development. The supervising officer's personal dealings with the children may well be limited, but he will have their well-being very much in mind in the improvements that he tries to bring about.

Finally, he may decide to work for, rather than directly with, children who become caught in the cross-fire of bitter parental disputes over access. In some cases this will be because they are too young and immature or too limited in their verbal skills to be able to explain their feelings and their wishes to him. In others, where there is the promise of more fluent communication, he may still consider it unwise to involve them too closely. This will apply particularly in the decision-making stages, when the burden of apparent choice may be more than their limited sense of security can tolerate. Even where some personal counselling is attempted, it will almost certainly be secondary to the main task of conciliation with the parents. The primary problem being one of parental attitudes, the children will stand to gain more in the long run from changes achieved in this area than from any short-term supportive work which may be necessary with them.

It must still be remembered that the work is undertaken for the children's benefit. The success or failure of counselling with their parents can only be judged by the results it produces for them. Their reactions must always be carefully observed, however slight their own participation may be.

The participating child

In the majority of cases the child does participate actively in supervision. These are the cases in which he is old enough to have some appreciation of the significance of his parents' divorce and is able, as a result of his involvement in the welfare enquiry, to associate the supervising officer with this aspect of his life. The situations in which active work with the child is appropriate relate back to the emotional criteria for recommending supervision. Again, they fall into three main categories.

The first involves problems in personal relationships. The child can encounter a variety of such difficulties after divorce, and they can seriously hamper his integration in the emergent family unit. They may be with the custodial parent, the second partner or the second partner's children, and they can also occur in the extended family. They will not necessarily reflect a failure or an inability on the child's part to adjust to his new situation, since they can equally be symptomatic of parallel difficulties in the person with whom he finds himself in conflict. In either eventuality the supervising officer will need to work both with the child and the other protagonist to help them sort out their perceptions of each other's role and to modify their demands upon and responses to each other.

Second, there may be problems of inappropriate adjustment. The child, no less than his parents, needs his defences against the trauma of marital breakdown and these may on occasion be inappropriate to the point of hampering his future emotional development. He too will experience a period of mourning for the family which has been broken up, and he will find great difficulty in coping with it if his parents are too caught up with their own distress to provide him with the support and comfort he needs. He may then become withdrawn and introspective, trapped in the mourning phase in much the same way as the underfunctioning parent can fail to emerge from the initial period of depression and damaged confidence. The hurt of severed or altered relationships may ultimately prevent him from risking so full a commitment to seemingly loving adults again.

A similar situation is the one in which the child becomes too dependent emotionally upon his remaining parent. The circumstances will often be such that the parent, in fulfilling his own needs, either connives at this dependence or seeks actively to foster it. It is then that the child is most vulnerable to the transmission of distorted values and may build up inappropriate models for his future inter-sexual relationships.

The direct counselling which is called for in such situations is more difficult because the child is less than normally susceptible to outside adult influences, which he is learning in effect not to trust. These difficulties will be aggravated when, as in the second type of case, the supervising officer may be attempting to build a relationship against a background of suspicion or even open hostility on the part of the custodial parent.

Finally, there is access. In the majority of access problems, in which the child is old enough to have some conception of what the matter is about, some measure of direct counselling will be appropriate. The circumstances in which too active a participation should not be encouraged have already been outlined. There will be many other situations, however, in which the child will be only too anxious to express his opinions, and not least when he is strongly opposed to the idea of access.

The gradations between very limited counselling and a substantial investment in direct work with the child will be controlled partly by his age and his emotional capacity to sustain such a potentially demanding programme, and partly by his parents' probable reactions to its inception. The supervising officer can only focus his attention on exploring and understanding the child's feelings after he has established a reasonable rapport with the parents. He should not start to work at any depth with the child until he is sure that this will not create problems for him, in terms of undue pressures from his parents.

Problems of Supervision

The problems of matrimonial supervision are in many ways similar to those of divorce court welfare work in general. They include working with people who are unfamiliar with the client role and who are unwilling to accept it; dealing with the resistance of parents who feel that help has been offered too late and from a stigmatizing source; and accepting, as a worker, that situations have to be faced which strike uncomfortably close to home in a personal sense. These difficulties are frequently heightened in the transition from welfare enquiry to supervision order, and there are additional complications in terms of client definition which, if not unique, are at least more pronounced in this area of work than in any other.

Definition of the client

The problem of defining who is the client and then acting upon it is amply demonstrated by the almost bewildering choice of focus which is available to the supervising officer. The child named in the order is ostensibly the client, but it is very hard to help him without the cooperation of the custodial parent at least. In social work terms, either or both of the parents may be the effective client, with little direct involvement on the child's part. Yet the demands that can be made on the parents in a legal sense are virtually non-existent. If they choose not to accept help or not to allow the child to accept it, there are no effective sanctions to bring to bear. The nature of the order limits progress to what the parents can be persuaded to accept. The implications for the supervising officer and the additional demands upon his social work skills are considerable.

Parental resistance

Parental resistance to supervision is usually most acute in the case of middle-class families who have had no involvement with a social work agency prior to the welfare enquiry. It stems from two main sources.

First, there is the problem of stigma. Parents who feel affronted by the need for a welfare enquiry in the first place are likely to look even more askance upon any suggestion that supervision is required. They will frequently interpret it as a slight upon their abilities to care adequately for their children and if they are people of normal social competence and perhaps of some professional distinction they may be most reluctant to accept their need for help.

The feeling of stigma is compounded by the fact that the child is placed under the supervision of a probation officer, with all the connotations of criminality which this conjures up. The sense of bruised dignity and sometimes indeed of actual outrage can be long lived, even where it is the welfare officer who conducted the enquiry who continues to supervise.

It is perhaps a pity that the order is not termed a counselling order, with the court welfare officer nominated to implement it. This would do no more than reflect the process which actually takes place, and its greater acceptability in the eyes of the parents would often get it off to a distinctly happier start.

The second major cause of resistance lies in the time lag before a supervision order can be made. Just as many parents will feel at the enquiry stage that the welfare officer has come too late upon the scene, when the first and most painful adjustments have already been made, so too will they resent even more strongly the imposition of a supervision order some weeks or months later, when the issue in dispute has been dealt with by the court. Careful preparation at the enquiry stage will minimize this reaction, but it will not prevent it entirely. It is, after all, only too easy to understand. First adjustments have been made, and not without some anguish. For them to be challenged on the grounds that they are not in the child's interests, when no concern had been expressed for him at all at the highly traumatic point of breakdown, may seem like hypocritical hindsight.

It is understandable too that the parent should not perceive how strongly defensive his reaction is. His desire simply to preserve what element of hard-won stability he has achieved for himself and his child may seem to him to be wholly reasonable. So too may be his wish to be left to cope alone, as he had of necessity been obliged to do before. The burden of being forced to face up consciously to the implications of his present handling of the situation, and perhaps of revaluing his performance in the light of hitherto unconsidered factors, is scarcely one he will relish. The supervising officer needs to tread a delicate path between engaging him in the process of necessary reconsideration, and leaving as complete as possible the defences which may be essential to his survival in the parent role.

The worker threatened

Divorce court welfare work poses its own peculiar threats to the probation officer because it frequently strikes all too personal chords. Supervision will often add to his anxieties.

He has not only to continue to work for what may be a long time in this fraught arena, but he has often to start by helping parents and children to adjust to a situation which he has had a substantial part in bringing about. To some of those involved, the decision reached will have been distressing and seemingly unjust, and he will scarcely expect to escape their anger for all that it was the court which made the order. Convinced as he may be that the decision was in the child's best interests, he will still not be immune to the passions aroused by it. The task of conciliation will be one of the most challenging tests of his professional skills. The fact that his own emotions will inevitably be involved to some extent will not make it any easier.

7

Violent Families

The divorce court welfare officer will in the course of his work encounter many families in which domestic violence has been or still is a predominating feature. It will usually take the form of violence between husband and wife, but there will also be instances of assaults by parents upon children. The literature upon both wife battering and child abuse is extensive and familiar. The limited examination of these topics which follows is not intended to be exhaustive. It is restricted to those aspects of the accepted profiles of violent parents and partners which seem especially relevant to the field of divorce court welfare. The legal provision for dealing with violence within the family will also be reviewed, as well as the role of the welfare service in this context.

FAMILY VIOLENCE AND DIVORCE

It is impossible to determine how many marriages end in divorce as a result of violence between the partners; many more, certainly, than those in which violence is cited in petitions based on unreasonable behaviour. A two-year separation may provide the basis for an agreed divorce where consent would have been withheld had unreasonable behaviour been alleged. Where consent is not forthcoming in any event, it may still be easier as well as much less painful to establish the fact of a five-year separation than to prove that violence has taken place. Adultery may mask a similar situation, whether it is the assaulted wife who petitions on grounds which are more acceptable to her husband, or whether, having escaped from the violent relationship, she is content to allow his petition to proceed undefended.

Sometimes custodial parents are violent towards their children. In some cases this will be the continuation of a pattern of behaviour already established before the ending of an unhappy marriage. In others, where there is no previous history of ill-treatment, it will be a reflection of the emotional damage the divorce has caused or of the stresses of single parenthood.

The factors which contribute to marriage failure and to the inability of some parents to manage their families after divorce do seem to overlap to a significant extent with the now recognized determinants of family violence. They can be considered in relation to violence between partners, violence towards children, and those families in which violence appears to be endemic.

Violent Relationships

In violent marital or quasi-marital relationships it is usually but not invariably the man who is the aggressor and the woman the victim. Despite the publicity of recent years, the full extent of the problem remains uncertain because many women are still reluctant to reveal the fact that they have been assaulted. This applies particularly to wives in the upper socio-economic group.

The Welfare Service is recognized, by some at least, as having a legitimate counselling role in respect of such difficulties. Its assistance is, however, most commonly sought by the courts in those cases where children of the family are at possible risk. It is therefore appropriate to consider the risk to which children may still be exposed, even when they are not the deliberate and primary target of domestic violence.

The violent husband

Violent husbands have been characterized[1] as 'badly brought up men', spoilt or indulged during a childhood in which they had probably witnessed some measure of family violence. They have a low tolerance of frustration and are extremely dependent, often being unable to look after themselves. Alcohol constitutes their most commonly recurrent problem, with pathological jealousy and compulsive gambling also featuring repeatedly; factors which inhibit communication, including physical disabilities such as deafness, are also considered to be significant.[2]

These are men who lack satisfactory models for their own marital relationships. They resent their dependence on their wives at the same time as they perpetuate it by their continuing self-indulgence. They seem in their extreme and unreasoning jealousies to acknowledge their own inadequacies, and it is not surprising that they should seek persistently for reconciliations. There is, however, an element of acceptance that such reconciliations will not be long lasting, as if they recognize in themselves the poor candidates for matrimonial survival which in truth they are.

Two main patterns of violence have been identified in these husbands:[3] those who assault both their wives and their children, and those who accidentally cause injury to their children in the course of their attacks upon their wives.

Children of all ages are at direct risk from the violence of their fathers, even when they are not the intended victims. They may be babies who happen to be in their mothers' arms at the moment of attack, toddlers who are literally underfoot during the incident or older children who seek, however ineffectually, to intervene. Whatever reassurances their mothers may offer to the contrary, they can never in fact be completely safe in regularly violent households.

There is a further and specific element of risk for children who live in violent homes. Both Gayford[4] and Selwyn Smith quote evidence to suggest that wives who are repeatedly assaulted by their husbands do in a significant proportion of cases proceed in their turn to assault their children. If spared both deliberate and accidental injury at the hands of their fathers, the subsequent risk of assault by their mothers is considerable.

Unconscious provocation

One category of assaulted wives calls for particular mention – that of women who escape from one violent relationship only to enter into another with a partner who displays the same tendencies. Some at least of these women do acknowledge their role in provoking their partners' violence. Any theory which recognizes the possibility of such a pattern of behaviour tends to be received with hostility by women's groups and by many others who seek to help battered wives. This is readily understandable since these women are the exceptions. The majority of victims neither seek nor provoke the physical assaults to which they are subjected and their distress in the face of them at both a physical and an emotional level is manifest. Nevertheless, as Brandon states:

> those women who, despite adequate intelligence and access to information, become pregnant to and marry a man who has demonstrated his violence before marriage, survive years of physical assault, then separate only to repeat the cycle with another violent man, must be directed by unconscious motives or maladaptive learning patterns.[5]

The number of such women may be small, but it is important that they should be identified by the Welfare Service because of the risk to their children. This risk, as has been seen, may emanate from the new partner or may be at the hands of the mother herself. Where it is clearly established that a mother has been used with repeated violence in more than one relationship, there must be some danger of her finding herself in similar difficulties in the future. This possibility will not serve to disqualify her from continuing to care for her children, but supervision will obviously be a sensible precaution.

These cases in which a mother moves on to a second or subsequent violent relationship serve also to emphasize yet again the importance of the character and background of second partners in welfare investigations. The knowledge in cases of this kind that the new partner has a history of marital or other violence may well be central to the welfare officer's evaluation of the children's circumstances. It is quite unacceptable that he should not have access to such information.

Violent Parents

The mother

The mothers who are most likely to assault their children, other than the special cases of the mentally ill and subnormal, are young and immature women. They are frequently the children of failed and violent marriages who have been deprived of love and are unable to form sustained adult relationships. Their own capacity to give love is limited and their craving for affection unanswered. Significantly, in the context of divorce, they tend to be most vulnerable when they are under stress and their self-esteem both as women and as mothers is low.

This description overlaps to a remarkable extent with the profiles of the underfunctioning and inadequate mothers in the post-divorce situation. There are the familiar stigmata of failed adult relationships, damaged self-image as a woman and lack of self-confidence as a mother. It is almost a blueprint for the reaction to marriage failure, even though the final separation will in many cases not yet have taken place. Their already limited performance will almost certainly deteriorate still further with the additional stress of separation and divorce when it occurs, and the risk to the children will be intensified accordingly.

Where there is a known history of assault by the mother there will probably be some form of supervision already in being. The reporting welfare officer should confer with the supervisor to ensure that all the relevant information is put before the court. He should also ascertain whether any proposed recommendation would conflict with the supervising agency's plans for the mother and her child. He will rarely find it necessary in practice to propose a course of action which would run counter to such plans. He must, however, make it known to the court if he should arrive at a substantially different view as to where the child's best interests lie.

The welfare officer has a more crucial responsibility where there has been no previous social work involvement and he has to identify actual or potential abuse alone. These are often cases in which the mother's former ability to cope has broken down under the pressures of separation and divorce. Sometimes the identification will not prove difficult. The mother's history will provide some pointers; her ability to tolerate the demands of her children and to meet them appropriately will offer others. There may be clear danger signals, such as the characteristic demand for positive and loving responses from small babies, or obviously unrealistic expectations of very young children. Repeatedly expressed doubts and the constant need for reassurance as to her maternal capabilities may be significant. Any expression of fear that she might injure her child must always be taken seriously.

In other cases the warning signals may be harder to recognize. Standards of day to day care may be high, almost obsessionally so at times, and there may be a misleading veneer of competence. The violence may be episodic, broken up by periods of loving care during which the child responds to her affectionately and without fear. It may indeed be only the history of the mother and of the marriage which gives any cause for anxiety. The welfare officer must not allow himself to be satisfied too readily that all is well. Whenever there is a *prima facie* case for suspecting child abuse, he must as a standard practice discuss the case with a senior colleague.

The father

The portrait of the battering father presented by Brandon seems if possible to have an even more direct relevance in the context of divorce. He is described as a man who on occasion

> found the responsibility of caring for a small child intolerable, owing to the curtailment of freedom, incompetence in child care or intolerance of the child's failure to respond in a way which he expected. Faced with the care of the child, often in itself carrying implications of changed or inferior status, he experienced intense frustration which he expressed by inflicting pain, sometimes on himself and sometimes on the child.[6]

The potential dangers of this situation are the greater because violent fathers are generally recognized as being more likely to suffer from serious personality disorders than their female counterparts. Their assaults too are more likely to result in multiple injuries to the child.

The risks inherent in leaving children, and especially small children, in the care of such a father are obvious. They will clearly be increased after divorce by his relative isolation as a single parent, by his loss of employment on occasion, and by his frustration as he attempts to cope permanently with a child care function which it may be beyond his ability to discharge. Once again, the danger signals may be obvious, or they may be quite effectively disguised. The welfare officer must be alert to the possibility of abuse if he finds a father inexperienced in child management left to cope unaided with young and demanding children. A realistic awareness of potential risk does not imply a distrust of the 'mothering' capabilities of all abandoned fathers: it is only a due professional recognition of one particular area of difficulty with which any father so situated may be faced.

Endemic Family Violence

There is one group specifically identified in the literature on family violence which the welfare officer may meet with some regularity in his enquiries. This is that group of families through which, amid their proliferation of social problems, there runs a thread of repeated and serious physical violence. It is such as to bring its members before the criminal as well as the divorce courts, but neither are able to offer solutions to the problems that are presented. They are usually well known to a variety of social work agencies, but they seem to derive little benefit from the resources that are expended upon them. The children, often as violent as their parents, remain at serious risk both physically and emotionally for as long as they remain in their charge. In their more florid presentations, they can offer examples of almost every manifestation of domestic violence within the confines of a single family.

> At the centre of one such family is Joyce, apparently intent in her mid-thirties upon perpetuating indefinitely the atmosphere of naked violence which has been an integral part of her whole adult life. A big, crudely aggressive woman of limited intelligence and formidable physical presence, she has been known to the welfare service for some 10 years, since she first applied for the custody of her four young children. She had presented then as an erratic and heavy-handed but still affectionate and caring mother. Her original complaints had been of her husband's drunkenness and violence towards her. Subsequent events proved that she was equally violent physically, and had an even greater drinking problem. She had also complained of an indecent assault by her hus-

band on their oldest daughter, then aged 12,[7] and of her 10 year old son's increasingly violent behaviour.

A series of uneasy reconciliations followed, during which counselling achieved little. Pat, the son, was placed under supervision for assault and Joyce continued to drink very heavily. She made two suicide attempts before being placed on probation with a condition of in-patient psychiatric treatment for being drunk and disorderly. Here her marriage finally ended. The children were taken into care where they remained for several months. Joyce was then discharged unceremoniously from hospital after attacking a fellow patient. She seemed to have made little progress, but she managed to come to terms with her drinking problem without further medical help.

She insisted on the children's immediate return to her, although both Pat and Sandra, the oldest girl, were showing signs of acute disturbance and were quite beyond her powers of control. Verbal aggression and physical violence were simply matched in kind. Sandra took to prostitution and was committed to care, pregnant and totally rejected by her mother. Pat's committal soon followed, after a further conviction for assault. A period of relative stability ensued, with Joyce nearly able to cope with the two passive and amenable younger girls. Financial and employment crises there continued to be in plenty, for this was still very much a problem family, but physically there was peace.

At this stage Joyce took a cohabitee. Charlie admitted to a criminal record and he quickly demonstrated a propensity for violence even greater than her own. Abused and frightened as she was, however, she refused to make him leave. Pat returned home, lost the inevitable trial of strength with Charlie and progressed, via a brief and violent sojourn with his father, to detention. His next return had barely time to be tested before he was sent to prison for a serious offence of wounding at a football match.

Joyce's divorce was finally heard and the ensuing welfare enquiry prompted her to disturbing revelations about Charlie. A pornography-addicted voyeur, he was said to be exhibiting a most unwholesome interest in Joyce's two remaining daughters. Their allegations included attempts to watch them undress, minor indecent assaults, and repeated threats of corporal punishment which were clearly sexually and indeed sadistically motivated. Charlie denied all, but faced with the choice between him and her daughters, Joyce finally and apparently thankfully got rid of him. Both girls were nonetheless placed under supervision by the divorce court.

The precaution proved a wise one. After a year of tearful

pleading Charlie was restored, Joyce's frankly admitted sexual needs as well as a lingering affection for him finally deciding the issue. Both girls, prompted by their mother, withdrew all their previous allegations and with no proof of impropriety against him, he was allowed to remain. The older of the two then progressed to an adolescence all too much in the family tradition. Inevitably pregnant, she was admitted to care for her own safety; Joyce's infuriated threats of murder could well have resulted in tragedy. Her younger sister also accompanied her, Joyce having by then lost all inclination and ability to cope with her family further.

Any attempt to differentiate between the welfare and the criminal elements of enquiry and supervision in this case is to some extent artificial, since only one probation officer was involved with the family throughout. It is, however, typical of such cases that both aspects of his work were so fully represented. The welfare function stands out here both as the initial reason for the Service's involvement and as the trigger which later prompted the revelation of Charlie's full repertoire of aberration, and enabled a continued oversight thereafter through the girls' supervision orders.

It is also typical of such cases that a decade of almost continuous supervision had achieved so little. Joyce was left with little to look forward to beyond a relationship of continued violence with Charlie and with as full a confirmation as she could have feared of her failure as a mother. The children had all too clear a prospect of repeating in their turn the pattern of failed and violent relationships in which they had been raised. The wisdom of hindsight suggests that they would have been better served had they been removed much earlier from their mother's erratic and ultimately destructive influence.

THE LAW AND VIOLENT FAMILIES

Social attitudes towards family violence depend very much upon who is the sufferer. Violence towards children has become a matter of public concern in recent years, not least because of the intensive coverage given by the news media to cases in which children have been seriously injured or have died. The issue is seen, perhaps a little naively at times, in absolute terms of black and white, in which the child is the innocent victim and the aggressor a monster lacking any redeeming features. There is no doubt in the public mind that children need protection and no shortage of criticism for the social work agencies held to be responsible when tragedies do occur.

The same is not true in the case of the battered wife. She is seen as being better able to fend for herself, with the option, however unrealistic it may sometimes be in fact, of walking away from the violent situation should she choose to do so. Her problems receive less attention from the media, and the espousal of her cause by some of the more militant elements of the women's movement has not always been to her advantage. Public opinion is less willing to recognize wife battering as a significant social problem and, as is sometimes found in the case of the rape victim, the woman is seen in some undefinable fashion as being to some extent the author of her own misfortune.

The battered husband is a rare phenomenon and his existence is even less readily accepted. His status in the public view is almost that of a music hall joke, in the long tradition of humour based upon hen-pecked husbands and their formidable wives. The lack of sympathy for his plight is due less to indifference than to incredulity.

The present state of the law on family violence mirrors public opinion reasonably accurately. The law has long provided adequate protection for children and this has been reinforced with a wealth of procedural guidance in the wake of well-publicized tragedies. The civil law as it relates to violence between married partners, and indeed unmarried ones, is more confused and more cumbersome, with immediate and effective protection less easy to obtain. Such recent reforms as there have been have improved the situation, but it is still less than completely satisfactory.

Violence towards Children

The basic protection for children is to be found under the first section of the Children and Young Persons Act 1969.

Proceedings can be brought by the police or the local authority before a juvenile court under section 1(2)(a) in respect of a child who is himself being neglected or ill-treated. Section 1(2)(b) extends the protection to children living in the same household who may be at similar risk. Further protection is provided under section 1(2)(bb)[8] against adults who are, or are about to become, members of the household, and who have relevant convictions for offences against any children, whether or not they are also members of the household.[9]

Emergency provision, where the risk is too immediate to await a juvenile court hearing, is made under Section 28(1) of the Children and Young Persons Act 1969. A place of safety order allows for a child to be detained on the authority of a magistrate who is satisfied that a necessary condition for the bringing of care proceedings (other than the commission of an offence) exists in respect of him. Care proceedings must then be started within 28 days if the child is not released. Section 32(1A)[10] provides for the recovery of a child unlawfully removed from a place of safety in the same way as if he were the subject of a care order.

The juvenile court, upon finding the case proved, may make the child the subject of a care order, a supervision order or a hospital order. It may also require the parent or guardian to enter into a recognizance in respect of the care and control to be provided for the child in the future.

Violence towards Wives

The first priority in the case of a wife who has been assaulted by her husband is to provide her with protection against any repetition of the attack. It is therefore essential that there should be a swift and effective legal process through which she can be confident of obtaining such protection. The problem which then arises is that the provision of such immediate protection, essential though it is in the short term, may militate against the processes of conciliation and reconciliation which the law will also wish to promote. It is a recognized fact that many assaulted women do return relatively quickly to their partners, and the danger of a legal process which tends to stigmatize the husband for his behaviour is that it may actually contribute to further discord and violence. This is a difficulty to which there is no obvious answer, since the law must provide the full protection which is the women's unquestionable right, even though she may only require it on a temporary basis. It is perhaps a function of the court's Welfare Service to reduce as far as possible the potentially adverse side-effects which may result from a necessary protection order.

For the wife who has been assaulted and who wishes to take action against her husband there are two main courses open. She may seek a prosecution under the criminal law or she may institute proceedings in a civil court. In the latter case she may start the process through which her marriage will be permanently ended, or she may seek the protection of an injunction; in some circumstances a combination of these two processes may be necessary.

Criminal prosecution

Criminal proceedings against husbands for assault upon their wives are relatively uncommon, except in cases where very serious injuries result. Wives may be reluctant to prefer criminal charges for a variety of reasons. Some will see it as an effective bar to the reconciliation for which they still may hope. Others may fear that retribution would follow upon such a step. It must be remembered that the husband is unlikely to be imprisoned unless the offence is a particularly grave one and that the wife, short of instituting further civil proceedings, will more often than not be left without any legal protection after his conviction. Some wives, despite their injuries, will still see the matter as an essentially private and domestic one and will consider it inappropriate for their husbands to be branded as criminals as a result of their behaviour.

A further difficulty for wives who wish to prefer criminal charges is that the police are often reluctant to prosecute in the case of relatively minor assaults. This is because many women fail to go through with the proceedings when the immediate crisis has been resolved with the husband's removal. It is obviously both time-consuming and frustrating to detain and charge a man, only to find the following morning that the sole witness has withdrawn her complaint. The traditional low profile of the police in domestic matters is not hard to understand. Neither is their reluctance to become formally involved unless they are satisfied that the wife is in genuine danger.

Separation and divorce

The wife who decides as a result of her husband's violence that she wishes permanently to leave him can institute proceedings for divorce or for a matrimonial order as a long term remedy.

If other accommodation is available for her and the children and she is in no danger of further violence whilst the court hearing is awaited, she may need no further protection. This is not, however, the typical situation. The problems of finding alternative accommodation are usually acute, especially where there are children, and many wives have to start proceedings before they leave their husbands. This decision will in itself provoke further violence in many cases and there will be a need for formal legal protection. The same will be true for the wife who, having moved out, is threatened with further harrassment when her husband discovers where she is living.

The injunction

The wife who needs protection after the institution of divorce proceedings has long been able to obtain it by means of an injunction in the county court. The same remedy is now also available to wives who do not wish to end their marriages, but are still in need of temporary protection from their violent husbands.[11]

Section 1 of the Domestic Violence and Matrimonial Proceedings Act 1976 empowers the judge to grant an injunction restraining a husband (or wife) from molesting the applicant or any child in the applicant's charge. The respondent can also be excluded from the matrimonial home and prohibited from entering the locality in which it is situated.

The Act does not specify that the applicant must have filed or must undertake to file a petition for divorce before an injunction can be granted. Protection is available to all wives, whether or not they intend to separate from their husbands. Prospects of both conciliation and reconciliation must be enhanced now that divorce proceedings do not have to be started in order to qualify for the court's protection.

Under Section 2 of the Act the judge may attach a power of arrest to the injunction if he is satisfied that an incident has already occurred as a result of which the applicant or a child has suffered actual bodily harm. This gives the police the authority to arrest the respondent without a warrant in the event of a breach of the injunction. Whilst this represents a considerable improvement upon the previous position, in which the police had no power of arrest at all, it still does not provide adequately for the wife who is only threatened with violence. The effect in practice is that some measure of physical injury has to be sustained before a worthwhile protection becomes available.

The protection afforded to wives under both these sections of the Act is also extended to women who live with but are not married to their violent partners. The implications are considerable, especially in terms of property, since a man can now be excluded from his own home in favour of a woman who is not his wife. This provision has been hailed in some quarters as a 'mistresses' charter', but it seems doubtful whether the Act as interpreted by the courts will provide them with as ready an access to their partners' property as is apparently envisaged.[12] The implied principle, that all women are entitled to the same protection in law regardless of their marital status, is surely unexceptionable.

From a welfare point of view, the Act is less than comprehensive. There is no provision for the ordering of welfare reports, which are often felt to be necessary in cases of family violence. More seriously, there is no provision either for the making of care or supervision orders in respect of the children of the family, who may as has already been seen be at considerable risk. In the anxiety to protect women against assault, admittedly the primary purpose of the Act, the needs of their children have been largely overlooked. It has been held that the general provision of Rule 95(1) of the Matrimonial Causes Rules 1977 is a sufficient authority for the ordering of a welfare report if there are children of the family, and this would appear sound. A report by itself, however, is of little help to the court if it lacks the power to take action in the children's interests. Such action is only possible at present if there is a simultaneous custody application under the Guardianship of Minors Acts.

The injunction procedure, however, does have its limitations. The judge who attempts to provide an assaulted wife with an appropriate measure of immediate protection without infringing any further than is essential upon the rights that the husband still possesses must always be faced with some difficulty. The initial application is of crucial importance and when it is made *ex parte* (see note 4.2, page 192) it may be impossible to reconcile these two conflicting demands. An immediate order in favour of the wife may be essential and she may also establish an excellent case for an exclusion order. The court will be reluctant to order a man from his own home forthwith, without having heard his account of events. This can lead to an uneasy compromise in which an anti-molestation order is made without an exclusion order, in an attempt to contain the situation against a full hearing a few days later. The atmosphere in the home is bound in that time to become more highly charged than ever. Even if the wife is saved from further actual violence – and this will not invariably be the case – she will have to suffer a situation in which she may feel herself to be at as great or even greater a risk than she was initially. It is right that courts should be cautious about expelling men from their own homes even in a final order, but many wives will question the value of a documentary protection which still leaves them sharing the same house as their violent husbands.

An unfortunate side effect of the injunction, especially when an exclusion order is sought, is that many husbands will interpret it as an attempt to secure possession of the matrimonial home, rather than as one to prevent further physical violence. One reason for this is that few husbands find it possible after the event to admit the extent of their assaults. Where the reaction is not one of total denial it will frequently be one of minimizing the violence and perhaps of attempting to justify it in terms of the conduct which provoked it. A husband who is convinced of his wife's ulterior motives in seeking an exclusion order may respond by applying himself for the custody of the children, a step which he would probably never have contemplated but for the threat to his home. A husband with a proven propensity for violence is unlikely to gain the custody of his children, but the simple fact of his application will usually cause much anxiety and distress both to them and to his wife.

The injunction is a basically unsophisticated remedy, designed to deal with the crisis of domestic violence or the immediate threat of it. There is, unfortunately, no distinction in its application as between the wife who needs long-term or permanent protection against the possibility of very serious assault, and the one who is seeking only a temporary relief in the context of a marriage which may yet be retrievable. The full rigours of the law which are necessary in the first instance may be quite inappropriate in the second and may indeed work actively against the possibility of a reconciliation.

An injunction remains in force, in theory, until an application is made for it to be discharged. Couples can, however, become reconciled and resume full cohabitation even where an exclusion order is still in being. This can sometimes seem to be a potent weapon to the wife who is unwise enough to use its threatened reactivation as a means of levelling the odds in the struggle for marital supremacy. The husband's position can rapidly become untenable, with a further eruption of violence the almost certain outcome. This abuse of the court's protection could be prevented if injunctions lapsed automatically within a given period after the resumption of cohabitation. Alternatively, they could be made for a defined period of three or six months and be renewable on application, subject to the court's satisfaction that the need for protection still exists.

Properly used, the injunction is the most effective remedy presently available to the assaulted wife. It is therefore important that it should not become devalued by too liberal use. It needs to be seen as a fair as well as an effective process. Then, paradoxically, it need not be a destructive influence upon threatened but still tenable marriages.

The personal protection order

The personal protection and exclusion orders introduced by the Domestic Proceedings and Magistrates Courts' Act 1978 make available through the magistrates court a measure of protection for assaulted wives which is broadly similar to that afforded by the county court injunction. This fills an evident need by bringing this type of protection readily within the reach of women whose place of residence denies them easy access to a county court.

It is perhaps unfortunate that the specific duty which is laid upon the court to consider the possibility of reconciliation before making an order for financial provision does not also obtain, at least on an optional basis, in the case of orders which relate to family violence. As many victims do in fact choose to return to their partners, it would have been appropriate to encourage a welfare intervention at this stage. Unsuccessful attempts at reconciliation, followed by the need for further protective orders, will in the end tend to devalue the process, as already happens at times with injunctions in similar cases.[13]

THE ROLE OF THE WELFARE SERVICE

There is at present no clearly defined role for the Welfare Service when domestic violence reaches that point of crisis at which the court becomes involved. There is a substantial body of opinion, including many representatives of the women's movement and a significant number of matrimonial lawyers, which would contend that the physical protection of the assaulted wife is the only relevant issue and that social work intervention at this stage is not appropriate. There is also some element of uncertainty within the social work profession as to how precisely the task of a court-based Welfare Service should be defined in this context. There are in consequence considerable variations in local practice, with much depending on the views held by individual judges and welfare officers. In some courts the service is scarcely called upon at all; in others it is used extensively, but not always consistently or appropriately. If there is in fact a need for social work help at the initial point of crisis – and this is not difficult to demonstrate – the nature of the help should not be too difficult to define.

The Present Welfare Task

Where the help of the Welfare Service is enlisted it is at present usually for one of three purposes: to provide emergency short term welfare reports; to arrange and sometimes to supervise access; or to offer a counselling service to the parties. These activities are not in themselves inappropriate, but they do not always relate sufficiently closely to the areas of need that can be identified; the service provided to the client, and possibly to the court, is in consequence less effective than it might be.

The emergency report

Emergency reports are usually called for when there are children of the family and the level of alleged violence in the home is such as to give serious cause for concern about their well-being. The level of anxiety as well as the level of risk to the children is likely to be high, and it is essential that all such reports should be produced quickly.

In some cases a divorce petition will already have been filed and an application for interim custody may then be combined with the injunction proceedings. This will enable the court to make whatever order is necessary in the children's interests and it will also provide a specific focus for the report. An interim report in these circumstances, providing the court with sufficient information upon which to base a temporary provision for the children, can be of considerable value. Although inevitably not exhaustive, it should be sufficient for example to establish that the mother has not herself been too damaged by her experience to be able to continue, at least for the present, as a safe and competent custodial parent. A conventional fully-fledged welfare enquiry can and should follow: the family situation will need to be more thoroughly assessed and the possibilities of effective conciliation work explored. Neither task can be undertaken in the first throes of the crisis and they should not indeed be embarked upon until the safety of both the children and their mother has been secured.

The task of the welfare officer in cases where there are no divorce proceedings will be broadly similar, provided that the injunction proceedings are accompanied by an appropriate custody application under the Guardianship of Minors Act. The welfare officer will not usually be required to offer direct comment upon the merits of the injunction application itself. Whether or not an order should be granted, and if so whether it should contain an exclusion clause, are matters for judicial determination rather than social work recommendations. The welfare officer can, however, assist the court to the extent of indicating what effect the various possible orders might be expected to have upon the children. This will enable the judge to keep the question of their welfare in mind whilst framing an order which still fulfils the primary function of protection from assault.

Access arrangements

Fathers against whom injunctions have been made often contest the issue of access strongly. Some are motivated by a genuine desire to see their children. Others attempt to use it as a method of maintaining contact with their wives. The children are usually protected by the injunction. Access can then take place only if the court introduces a saving clause to exclude it from the order. The father's case for including such a clause can be persuasive if the history of assault relates only to his wife, and the children are not unwilling to see him.

The court then has to weigh the best interests of the children, which may demand that access be permitted, against the possible risk to their mother of relaxing the terms of the injunction. The welfare officer has a central role in the attempt to balance this complex and potentially explosive equation. The first essential is a full and thorough welfare enquiry. The father is likely to press for a swift resolution. So too may the court if the judge, having excluded the father from the home, is anxious to provide him with such legitimate compensation as may be possible. These pressures should be resisted, for this is emphatically not an area for hasty decisions. Unless the welfare officer is allowed enough time to gain the full confidence of mother and children, the chances of achieving a satisfactory access relationship will be remote. Access imposed against their wishes can only be disastrous.

The whole concept of access is likely to be acutely threatening to the mother. She may need a variety of reassurances before she is able even to consider it. She will often insist, and wisely, that access does not take place at her home and does not involve her in any contact with her husband. This will secure her position against any planned abuse of the access facility in relation to herself. The use of a neutral hand-over point, with the children transported by a relative or a voluntary associate, will meet her requirements here. She may also wish for access to be fully supervised, and here it may prove more difficult to accommodate her. Supervision may be appropriate initially whilst anxieties are at their height, but it cannot be continued indefinitely. The final choice, as always, must be between unsupervised access and no access at all.

A further problem can arise if the mother agrees to access conditionally upon her address remaining secret. This places upon the children the intolerable burden of denying their father information which he may seek with some persistence. Access cannot be beneficial in such circumstances and it should be denied if it is indeed imperative that the mother's address should not be disclosed.

Counselling

Referrals for counselling, when they occur, tend to be made after the court has made its protection order. This is not the most favourable occasion for genuine conciliation work. It seems at such times that the Welfare Service is being asked only to persuade the husband to accept the court's decision and to stop making a nuisance of himself. Some courts are concerned only with purely practical issues, such as helping the husband to find alternative accommodation and to transfer his belongings after an exclusion order. Such mundane assistance may well be necessary, but it is a far cry from serious counselling with a view to conciliation.

The greatest problem with such referrals, and this is true of all too much of the present work of the Welfare Service in relation to domestic violence, is that they are not made until after the court has reached its decision. It is hardly surprising if this seems to the excluded husband like adding insult to injury. He is often likely to feel, and not without justification in the case of *ex parte* proceedings, that he has been judged without a fair hearing and has himself been the victim of an essentially one-sided process. This may be inevitable if proper priority is to be given to the protection of his wife, but it will not alter his feelings. He is all too likely to see any subsequent hearing as little more than a confirmation of a decision which has already been taken against him. When it is remembered that what many such husbands want is not conciliation but reconciliation, it is only to be expected that he will see the service which is finally offered to him as being too little and much too late.

The Need for Social Work Help

The case for social work intervention when situations involving marital violence first come before the court rests upon three propositions. These are that women who are the victims of sustained assaults need support and advice beyond their legal rights while they decide what remedy to seek; that the damage caused to potentially retrievable marriages by temporary but necessary legal protection should be reduced as far as possible; and that the polarizing effect inevitable in any legal proceedings should be minimized from the outset.

The right of the wife to immediate and effective protection is not challenged by any of these propositions. What is challenged is the widely-held assumption that its provision is inconsistent with the simultaneous offer of other forms of help. Successful counselling can reduce the need for continued protection. To be successful it must be started before attitudes have hardened to the point at which conciliation has become unattainable. When the climate created by the making of an injunction has become acceptable to either party it may already be too late.

Pre-hearing counselling

Repeated physical assault has an emotionally battering effect which can be as distressing and as debilitating as the injuries which it causes. A woman who is the recent victim of violence is often in a state of both physical and emotional shock which may prevent her from seeing anything beyond her own immediate distress. She will rarely be in a fit state to take decisions which could have far-reaching effects in the future for herself, her children and her marriage. Her only and wholly understandable reaction may be that she wants simply to escape from a situation which has become intolerable to her. The ways in which she can achieve this and the right to make use of them forthwith must be explained to her without equivocation. It is improbable, however, that she will not also stand in need of both practical and emotional support, and these too should be offered to her. The idea of longer-term counselling may be beyond her grasp at this point, or may appear wholly irrelevant, and it should not be pressed upon her. She can nonetheless be left with the knowledge that assistance is and will remain available to her whatever course of action she may decide upon.

Pre-hearing counselling will not always be limited to a statement of available help. Many wives are genuinely uncertain as to what they should do. Not all are happy at the speed with which their lawyers propel them along the path of litigation, as if no other course were possible. There can be tremendous advantage for the wife in even a single half-hour interview in such circumstances. It may not dissuade her from taking proceedings – it will not, indeed, be intended to do so – but it will leave her more aware of what she is doing, why she is doing it, and of the possible consequences of her chosen course of action. It will also leave the door open for further conciliation work.

Temporary separations

Large numbers of assaulted wives do return to their husbands relatively quickly, often following a repeating pattern of assault, separation and reconciliation over a period of months or years. Intermittent legal proceedings, including injunctions, provide no lasting solution. They serve only to erode the fabric of the marriage still further and perhaps even to increase the frequency with which the episodes of violence occur.

There would seem to be a particularly strong case for pre-hearing counselling when such a history exists. A wife is in no way less entitled to the court's protection upon a second or subsequent application and no attempt should be made to dissuade her from seeking it. She may, however, be less certain as a result of past experience as to whether this is the remedy she really wants. In some cases it will simply be that she is not aware of any alternative. The idea of counselling, whether or not she continues with the protection proceedings, may help her to look beyond the immediate crisis and really consider the future of her marriage.

Counselling, perhaps on the basis of a necessary initial separation, can have much to offer both husband and wife. Reconciliation need not necessarily be the objective, although the possibility will usually be implicit in the history. At the least, counselling will offer the opportunity for a positive decision. This must be preferable to an unplanned and often unconvinced surrender to the husband's insistence that he will mend his ways or to the defeated weariness which can no longer cope with the pressures of separate living. The inertia which produces this type of reconciliation is rarely based upon a belief that the marriage can or will succeed, and is all too often the prelude to further disharmony and violence.

Polarization

The polarization of attitudes which legal proceedings induce is a familiar problem in all aspects of matrimonial litigation. Its effect is perhaps more extreme in the field of domestic violence than anywhere else, because the wife is both initiator and prosecutor in a confrontation which admits of no compromise. It is inevitable that many wives should see the injunction application as a personal Rubicon and that the responses of their husbands should confirm them in that view. Their opinion seems, less happily, to have been shared by too many lawyers. The necessary legal dispositions are frequently made in an atmosphere of total hostility, which serves to make the gulf finally unbridgeable.

The more acute the need for protection, the more hostility the proceedings are likely to engender, and the more convinced the parties are likely to feel that there can be no going back. In many cases this will be no less than a recognition of the truth, but even where there is no going back there must still be some looking forward. Those who can no longer live together have to learn to accept that they must live apart, which is by no means the same thing. If there are children the parents must still be involved if only indirectly in each other's lives and in no circumstances can the past simply be obliterated. The scope for counselling with both parties is almost endless and it can modify attitudes so that orders are at least less likely to be breached. Again, if it is offered from the outset when responses are likely to be at their most explosive, it is likely to be most effective. Referral to the Welfare Service should be automatic upon the making of the protection order.

Crisis Intervention: a Viable Role

The common theme which has run through much of the discussion upon the social work role in domestic violence is that of help being made available at an early stage. Far from being inappropriate, this early involvement has been seen to be an important factor in the success of the counselling which follows. What is required therefore is a Welfare Service which can encompass crisis intervention in this area as a part of its normal working programme. Staff should be made available to see applicants as a matter of course both before and after injunction proceedings and to accept for immediate action referrals for welfare enquiries in cases where they are needed. It may be hoped that as such a system of early referral develops, it will be extended to include victims of domestic violence who approach the service for counselling before legal action is taken.

Crisis intervention of this kind will only be effective if it has the support of the legal profession and of the women's groups who are identified with the cause of the battered wife. The legal profession will need to be persuaded that help for the assaulted wife need not be restricted to formal legal protection, whilst the deep suspicion with which some of the women's organizations view court-based social work will have to be overcome. A radical change of outlook will be required on this second front. It would represent considerable progress in itself if the suspicions of the women's movement could be sufficiently allayed to allow it even to work in reasonable harmony with the Welfare Service towards what is, after all, their common goal.

Counselling

The services of a welfare officer should be available in any court in which injunction proceedings are listed. Applicants should be advised of the welfare officer's presence and encouraged to discuss their difficulties with him before going into court. It should be explicitly stated that this would not prejudice their right to proceed with the application in any way. Hearings should be so arranged that there is ample time for consultation before the case is called. Whilst there should be no formal requirement that applicants see the welfare officer, the court's expectation that they would normally do so would be conveyed.

In cases where an injunction is granted or an undertaking is entered into, the parties would be advised to see the welfare officer before leaving the court. The court would then be playing an active role in promoting the counselling process. It would be seen, by its referral, to be acknowledging the need for further assistance after the order is made, and its support for the conciliation attempt would be made explicit.

The role of solicitors would be of considerable importance, since the impact of this type of counselling would depend in part at least upon how positively it was presented by them. A greater understanding of the need for conciliation, coupled with a less blinkered perception of legal protection as the sole expedient, could lend it some real impetus. It could, on the other hand, be as completely emasculated as was the reconciliation provision in the Divorce Reform Act by a similar display of indifference.

Interim reports

It should be a recognized function of the Welfare Service to provide interim reports at short notice in cases where the court is satisfied that children may be at risk. This will occur most commonly when an interim custody application is combined with injunction proceedings. The referral should be seen as a holding operation, which is required to do no more than confirm that the immediate safety of the children is secured, against the later preparation of a comprehensive welfare report. The interim report will thus be both brief and narrowly focused. It will not be a substitute for the full enquiry, and any temporary expedients which it may propose should not be given more weight than they are intended to bear. Final recommendations must always wait upon the full enquiry.

Emergency enquiries of this kind are only appropriate in cases of possible risk to children. This will exclude some situations where family violence has been acute and where it is the principal issue before the court. An injunction may be sought, for example, where the parties are already separated and the mother's ability to care adequately for her children is established. Access or even custody may be in dispute, but if the children's immediate well-being is not in question, the issue does not need to be investigated on an emergency basis. It can and should be dealt with by means of a conventional welfare enquiry.

Direct referrals

The overall policy of the Welfare Service is to conciliate. It seeks, where it cannot prevent legal proceedings, to mitigate their damaging effects. It follows from this that it should undertake an advisory function for those who have not yet embarked upon formal proceedings. This function will be as relevant in the sphere of domestic violence as elsewhere, although the nature and the urgency of the problems involved will make its application less frequent.

A service should thus be offered – and be known to be offered – to victims and indeed to perpetrators of family violence before legal action has been decided upon. Direct referrals might come from a variety of sources. Some could come from parties who have had a previous contact with the Welfare Service, or from their acquaintances. Others could be from those who might find such an approach less threatening and in their eyes less final than a direct consultation with a solicitor. Others, when it is apparent that counselling is needed before decisions are taken, might be channelled through other social work agencies or even through the legal profession itself.

It should not be assumed that direct applications to the Welfare Service would necessarily imply a wish for counselling with a view to reconciliation. There would be many, perhaps a majority of clients, whose primary need and desire would be for physical protection, even if they wished first to talk through the implications of a proposed application. The welfare officer's task, besides helping to clarify the issues involved, would remain that of providing continuing emotional support and practical assistance.

8

Conclusions: The Future

The sweeping changes introduced by the Divorce Reform Act of 1969 have been assimilated with comparative ease within the course of the past decade. Divorce may not yet be completely acceptable in a social sense, but it is generally conceded that the legal dissolution of unions which are already dead in every other respect does not seriously threaten the institution of marriage. It is recognized too that the inevitable increase in the number of divorces does not necessarily mean that marriages are becoming inherently more unhappy or unstable. Insofar as this increase reflects more accurately the number of broken marriages which are acknowledged as such and terminated accordingly, it may be seen as a healthy rather than as a disturbing development.

The legal dissolution, however, is only a part of the ending of a marriage. The theme of conciliation which has run through this consideration of divorce procedures has lent repeated emphasis to the role of the court's welfare arm in helping to deal with the emotional and practical problems the parties so often face. If this is true for the adults who divorce, it applies with even greater force to the children who are the principal casualties. No system of legal adjudication can hope to meet at first hand the psychological consequences of the decisions which must be taken in their interests. The responsibility again falls largely to the Welfare Service.

It is appropriate to examine further this balance between legal adjudication on the one hand and the conciliation function of the Welfare Service on the other, since it is crucial to the quality of the provision that is made for children in divorce. On a somewhat broader front it is also material to consider the overall approach of our legal system to family matters. Central here are the problems implicit in our continuing pattern of dual jurisdiction and the desirability of adopting a unified system of family courts. The future of the Divorce Court Welfare Service is closely bound up with these considerations. It could, given a sufficient commitment, provide the basis for the family court welfare service of the future. Its present somewhat equivocal position on the fringes of the Probation and After-Care Service could in any event be modified to advantage.

CUSTODY AND ACCESS: ADJUDICATION OR CONCILIATION?

Issues of custody and access, put at their most simple, are about the regulation of family relationships following marriage breakdown. They involve continuing relationships not only between children and their parents, but also between the estranged parents themselves. It is notoriously difficult to legislate for relationships between people in any circumstances and it is tempting in this very sensitive and highly charged area of human experience to suggest that they cannot adequately be catered for by law. The personalized, confidential and flexible approach of social work practice may well be thought to have more to offer in terms of lasting and workable solutions than any formal legal pronouncements. The courts themselves are coming increasingly to acknowledge that some of the problems of disputed access, for example, are not really susceptible to legally imposed solutions.

Social work, even so, is no universal panacea. Many custody and access problems admit of no satisfactory solution, and the least damaging expedient may perforce have to be ordered in the face of the parties' refusal otherwise to accept it. Social work help can never achieve more than the clients are willing to allow. When conciliation has failed and all possibilities of compromise are exhausted, the recourse must then be to law. Its operation may not be perfect in an area not best suited to its traditional practices, but the right of every parent to seek its remedies must be unassailable. The due operation of law is also in a very real sense the right of the child as well. Even when his parents can arrive at a mutually acceptable accommodation, there must still be an external authority to ensure the proper protection of his interests.

Assuming then the need for a final and enforceable remedy at law, it is still necessary to find an appropriate balance between the legal process and other potential sources of help which may be equally effective in the long term and less traumatic in their immediate impact. The present system, in which the parties seek direct confrontation through the legal process as a first option rather than as a last resort, has failed thus far to find that balance. One which concentrated more exclusively on the children's interests in a setting less preoccupied with parental conflict would have much to commend it.

LIMITATIONS OF THE PRESENT PROCEDURES

Although custody and access have long been accepted as appropriate issues for judicial intervention, it is not unfair to suggest that neither lawyers nor legal administrators have been flexible enough in their approach to accommodate them to the best advantage. This criticism applies to the court setting itself, to the adversarial system under which the proceedings are conducted and to the selection and training of judges and advocates for this very specialized area of work.

The Court Setting

Custody and access hearings too often take place in buildings and in court rooms designed for quite different purposes. When accommodation is shared with criminal courts, and facilities for waiting and for consultation are inadequate and overcrowded, it is hard for parties to escape the conclusion that they are being accorded precisely the same consideration as the criminal clientele with whom they have no choice but to mix.

This impression can be reinforced by court rooms which, even if they are specifically designated for civil use, can still appear much too imposing and impersonal for the hearing of such private and emotive issues. The physical separation of the parties almost symbolizes the conflict between them, whilst the remote and isolated position of the judge adds to the impression that judgment is to be passed on them. The fact that the court is sitting in chambers may guard against actual intrusion, but it does little to dispel the parties' feeling that they are themselves on trial, and in an arena that is less than wholly private.

When judges do hold hearing in their rooms, and are literally as well as technically 'in chambers', the impact of the less formal setting is immediate. When the parties and their lawyers sit round the same table with the judge, some of the atmosphere of battle is dissipated and it becomes more possible to think in terms of seeking a solution together. The judge, though still clearly presiding, appears at this close range to be more actively involved and concerned and the parties, appreciably more at their ease, give a much truer and therefore more helpful account of themselves.

Genuinely private hearings of this kind should be the rule rather than the exception. They need not detract from the dignity and authority of the court and they can contribute positively not only to the civilized conducting of the proceedings, but also to the process of conciliation.

The Adversarial System

Much current criticism of the present handling of disputed custody and access issues centres upon the adversarial system under which the proceedings are conducted. Its polarizing influence is acknowledged and in concentrating too much upon the wishes of the parents and too little upon the welfare of the child, its effect on the prospects of conciliation is seen to be adverse.

Although the importance of conciliation has regularly and properly been stressed, the fact that many of those who divorce will continue in a state of bitter conflict is fully recognized. So too is the inevitability of their ensuing battles before the courts. To accept the existence of this conflict, however, is not to accept that it must be pursued through a divisive system which accentuates areas of disagreement instead of trying to capitalize on such common ground as may remain.

From a welfare point of view, the adversarial system is based upon a false premise. It assumes that the task is to present the case for each side in the most favourable light, rather than to seek objectively a solution which is in the best interests of the child concerned. An inquisitorial approach would be both more logical and more productive. Seeking only to establish the facts relevant to the child's welfare, it could then proceed to an adjudication based exclusively on this consideration.

The Appointment of Judges

Jurisdiction in divorce proceedings is shared between the Family Division of the High Court and the county court. The High Court has sole jurisdiction in defended divorce causes, whilst the county court deals with undefended divorces. Each court is responsible for the custody and access issues arising out of the proceedings before it, irrespective of whether these issues are themselves contested. Since the vast majority of divorces are undefended, it follows that most custody and access cases are heard in the county court.[1]

It is perhaps surprising in these circumstances that the judges who deal with family matters in the county court should not do so on a full-time and exclusive basis. Interest in and suitability for a family jurisdiction cannot be the sole criteria for selection when judges have other and unrelated duties to perform. It may well be thought that issues so fundamental to children's welfare deserve the high level of priority which a sole jurisdiction would imply.

The effective single focus of the Family Division presents no parallel difficulty. Such problems as there may be are probably inherent in its High Court status, since only judges of great experience are elevated to its ranks. The danger that they may find themselves distanced to some extent by age from the life styles of the children with whom they are called upon to deal will be the greater if their previous professional practice has been in fields remote from family law. The High Court bench has perhaps too little chance to benefit from the infusion of at least some of the views and values of a younger generation.

No ready solution presents itself in either situation. The

long-term answer might be found in the formation of a single and unified system of family law. Earlier and more effective specialization would be encouraged and from this there could emerge a cadre of fully experienced but still comparatively youthful full-time and specialist judges, such as is unlikely to evolve under the present system.

The Training of Advocates

Whilst there is some degree of specialization among both solicitors and barristers in family matters, it is not so widespread as might be expected, given the obvious social importance of the issues involved. Such specialization as does exist tends to be purely legal in scope, with little sophisticated appreciation of the emotional impact of the proceedings on parents and on children. Family law is not a popular area of legal practice, and at least some of the clients are in consequence less expertly served in their domestic affairs than when they seek legal advice and representation in other contexts.

A unified system of family law might, as has been suggested, provide the necessary impetus towards a more appropriate level of specialization. A greater emphasis might then be placed on training in the sociological and psychological aspects of divorce instead of viewing it in purely legal terms. Given a correspondingly heightened awareness of the lawyer's role on the part of the Welfare Service, the stage could be set for a more fruitful cooperation between the legal and social work professions. There is still too much distrust and too many misconceptions on both sides at present.

THE FAMILY COURT

The case in favour of a family court is based upon the proposition that there is inherent advantage in a unified and uniformly applied system of family law which can deal with all aspects of marital breakdown. The essence of this advantage is that it enables skilled and qualified personnel in the fields of both law and social work to develop specialized techniques for handling the legal and emotional problems in which it results. These techniques are designed to facilitate the process of conciliation between the parties, to safeguard the welfare of their children and to secure wherever possible an agreed resolution to the issues in dispute. They are further designed, where conciliation fails, to minimize the trauma of the ensuing legal process.

A Therapeutic Judicial Institution

The family courts which have been in operation for more than half a century in various parts of the United States have been developed side by side with American concepts of family breakdown as a social as well as a legal phenomenon. They have embraced not only divorce, custody and maintenance, but wife-battering, child abuse and juvenile delinquency as well. These have all been seen as matters for diagnosis and treatment as much as for legal adjudication. The court, with its supporting services, has developed into something almost akin to a social work agency as well as a legal tribunal.

Central to the concept of the family court as generally envisaged in this country, and especially by the Finer Committee,[2] is the idea of a court which is primarily a judicial institution. The applicant is first and foremost the subject of legal rights and the role of welfare, however important, is seen to be subsidiary. This is a sound principle, but adherence to it need not inhibit the scope of a very flexible social work intervention. Provided the principle of legal remedy by right is clearly understood, the whole process up to and including the court hearing, and indeed beyond it, can legitimately be regarded as a means of introducing parties to the possibilities of help. This constitutes no infringement of their legal rights and there is no reason why the court itself should not play an explicit role in promoting conciliation. A specifically therapeutic function of this kind need not compromise its standing as the judicial body ultimately responsible for administering the law.

Jurisdiction of the Family Court

The family court could have an all-embracing jurisdiction on the American model, covering every aspect of family breakdown; it could be restricted to dealing exclusively with broken marriage and its aftermath; or it could have a more broadly-based but still strictly civil jurisdiction, covering all proceedings relating to children and their families short of those involving criminal offences.

The third model appears to have the most to offer. It would avoid the problems of a mixed civil and criminal jurisdiction, but would still be radical enough in its effect to resolve many of the existing anomalies between the county, magistrates' and juvenile courts. Its jurisdiction would extend beyond the consequences of marriage breakdown to include adoption, and care and protection proceedings. The welfare principle applies equally to all these issues and it seems only logical that they should all be dealt with by the same judicial machinery. The base of expert and specialized knowledge in the existing civil judiciary and its welfare service would not have to be broadened to an unbridgeable extent to accommodate them.

A family court on this model would assume the jurisdiction at present exercised by the divorce courts and the magistrates' domestic courts in their entirety, together with the civil jurisdiction of the juvenile court. Its work load would not be so diversified as to be unmanageable, but the increased range of its responsibilities would be sufficient to justify its separate existence. It would put to optimum use the judicial, legal and social work expertise that it would attract, whilst its cohesive underlying philosophy would further enhance the quality of its service.

The Family Court Welfare Service

The welfare service to the family court might be provided either by the Probation and After-Care Service or by the local authority social services department. Alternatively, an independent service could be created for the purpose, perhaps under the auspices of the Lord Chancellor's Department. The Probation and After-Care Service is in many respects the natural candidate. It provides the existing welfare service to the divorce courts, it has proven ability in reporting in contested issues and its working relationship with the civil judiciary is well established. Against this is its long association in the public mind with the criminal law and its own uncertainty as to how far it should commit its limited resources to civil work at a time when its primary focus is ever more firmly on the containment of adult crime.

The local authority can point to its substantial experience in some of the areas of work in which the new court would be involved. This applies particularly to much of the present juvenile court work. It is, however, relatively inexperienced in custody and access reporting, it is less identified with court-based work in general and, perhaps crucially, it has very real limitations on its resources which could seriously impair its performance in what would be a new and specialized area of work.

A new service, tailored specifically to the needs of the new court, has considerable attraction. Its fully-committed staff, drawn from both agencies, would suffer neither from the taint of criminality which some fear would attach to the Probation and After-Care Service, nor from the local authority's potential embarrassment as an interested party. It could be integrated into a national pattern of civil law administration and so derive a distinctive identity and status which it would otherwise be denied. Against this is the disproportionate cost of establishing a new service which, it could be argued, would differ little in actual performance from either of the other possible agencies, given that they were adequately staffed for the purpose.

THE DIVORCE COURT WELFARE SERVICE

The Probation and After-Care Service became the statutory welfare agency of the divorce courts in 1958. In a period of little over 20 years the divorce court function has changed almost out of recognition. From a beginning where a tiny minority of the staff was able to deal comfortably with the occasional activity which the courts required, it has now developed to the point where it makes a very considerable demand upon the resources of the Service as a whole. The response to this much increased demand has been variable to say the least. Some areas have restricted their activities to their minimum legal obligation, whilst others have embraced the cause with an enthusiasm which has doubtless contributed to the increasingly sophisticated use the courts have made of them. There has in general been a greater appreciation in recent years of the value of the Service's contribution in the divorce courts, but there has also been a greater disposition to question the continued involvement of an essentially criminally orientated agency in civil work at all.

It is unfortunate that the Service should be to some extent divided on this issue at a time when firm decisions are needed about the nature of its future commitment. For although the movement towards family courts has been disappointingly slow since the impetus provided by the Finer Report in 1974, it does not seem unduly optimistic to anticipate their ultimate introduction. Substantial delay there may be, but neither the force of the arguments in their favour on welfare grounds nor the still divided and unsatisfactory state of family law in this country will admit of indefinite postponement.

Those concerned for the welfare aspects of family courts cannot therefore afford simply to wait upon events. The Probation and After-Care Service offers a case in point. It is bound to be closely involved, whether it provides the new welfare service itself or whether a separate organization is created. In either event the main body of the original staff is likely to be drawn from amongst the present specialist divorce court welfare officers. If the Service does decide that it wishes to undertake this new responsibility, it should even now be considering how best to give some immediate and tangible demonstration both of its commitment and of its potential performance. This it might do by establishing a fully specialized service to the existing divorce, domestic and juvenile courts which can be seen to be competent to take its place in the new organization from the moment of its inception.

A Specialized Welfare Service

The Probation and After-Care Service has not tended to look with any great enthusiasm upon the idea of a separated and more autonomous family welfare division. Reorganization on this scale would, however, be the *sine qua non* of any realistic preparation to service the future family courts. It is the only way in which the stigma of criminal association could finally be dispelled and it also offers the only hope of refining the requisite professional skills and sustaining them at a sufficiently high level.

Staffing would present no insurmountable problems. Some divorce court welfare officers at least could be expected to make a permanent career in civil work and others too would be willing to make a long-term commitment to it. For the rest, two likely methods of recruitment suggest themselves. The first would be a system of secondment from the mainstream of probation practice such as presently operates in relation to prison welfare. The second would allow for the introduction of suitable staff from other agencies, such as social services departments, on either a permanent or a seconded basis.

Duties of the Welfare Service

The new welfare service could not undertake immediately all the duties which would fall to it on the introduction of family courts, if only because of the present statutory obligations of the local authority. What it could do, however, would be to discharge all the existing civil responsibilities of the Probation and After-Care Service. It would thus prepare all welfare reports for the divorce and domestic courts, and supervise where appropriate. It would report and supervise where necessary in care and protection proceedings before the juvenile court. It would also undertake guardian *ad litem* duties in adoption applications and in proceedings for the revocation of care orders.

The demands on the Service would not be so formidable as might at first sight be supposed. No additional duties are being proposed and the drawing together of these associated obligations would in fact conserve resources rather than dissipate them. The wastage when all staff acquire specialist knowledge for only occasional use would be eliminated, as also would be the present uneconomic arrangement whereby supervisory grades are constrained to keep abreast of developments in law and practice for what must be fairly limited returns. The whole Service, in short, would benefit from this level of specialization.

The Probation and After-Care Service does have the resources to prepare itself to this limited extent for the advent of family courts. It has yet to demonstrate conclusively its commitment to doing so. If the commitment is forthcoming, it will be in a unique position to help shape a new era of court-based family work. If not, it can only look forward to the gradual erosion of its present obligations and ultimately to its complete withdrawal from the civil sphere. Both the Service and the future family courts would be the poorer for its departure.

Notes

CHAPTER 2: Reporter and Conciliator: the Dual Role

1 It is interesting to note that some family courts in the United States, of which Los Angeles is an example, do make a clear distinction between the two roles. The duties of reporter and of conciliator are never undertaken by the same worker. It is also interesting that priority is given to the task of conciliation, with the reporting role relegated to a secondary and relatively mundane position.

This distinction appears to be unnecessarily artificial. The combined role can create difficulties if, for example, the client wishes to keep confidential information provided for the conciliation but not for the reporting function. These are, however, far outweighed by the advantages to both court and client of working with single officers; not least of these is the added depth and quality of the report, which gets much closer to essential attitudes and feelings when it actually embraces the conciliation aspect. The difficulties can, in any event, be largely avoided if the welfare officer gives a clear and full enough explanation of his duties and objectives at the outset.

2 Pincus, L., 'How to help the bereaved', *Social Work Today,* vol. 6, no. 13, 2 Oct., 1975, pp. 392–8.

3 Hallett, Kathryn, *A Guide for Single Parents: Transactional Analysis for People in Crisis,* Celestial Arts, California, 1974, p. 7.

4 Ibid. p. 8.

5 See Court of Appeal judgment in Thompson v Thompson (1975) quoted in Halsbury's *Laws of England,* 3rd edn, vol. 15: 1455.

CHAPTER 3: Custody

1 This definition of a child of the family is more generous than that provided under Section 16(1) of the Matrimonial Proceedings (Magistrates Courts) Act 1960, which is limited to:

(a) any child of both parties; and

(b) any child of either party who has been accepted as one of the family by the other party.

It should also be noted that the magistrates' power to make an order for the legal custody of any child of the family under Section 2(1)(d) of the Act of 1960 is restricted to children under the age of 16.

The definition substituted by Section 58(1) of the Domestic Proceedings and Magistrates Courts Act 1978 is identical to that provided by the Matrimonial Causes Act 1973. The magistrates' jurisdiction is further brought into line with divorce legislation by Section 7(2)(a) of this Act, which allows for an order to be made for the legal custody of any child of the family who is under the age of 18.

CHAPTER 4: Access

1 Supervised access does not, of course, offer the only protection against unlawful removal. Rule 94(2) of the Matrimonial Causes Rules, 1977, requires that 'unless otherwise directed, any order relating to the custody or care and control of a child shall provide for the child not to be removed out of England and Wales without the leave of the court except on such terms as may be specified in the order'.

Rule 94(1) provides for either party to apply *ex parte* (in the absence of the other party and without requirement that he be notified) for an order prohibiting the removal of any child of the family who is under 18 out of England and Wales without the leave of the court. This prohibition can be backed up by administrative procedures through the Home Office, which alert ports and airports to the danger of possible removal.

2 See Goldstein, J., Freud, A., and Solnit, A. J., *Beyond the Best Interests of the Child,* The Free Press Macmillan Publishing Co. Inc., 1973.

3 Children Act 1975, sections 26 and 27.

CHAPTER 5: Reports to the Court

1 The welfare officer is usually involved in wardship proceedings which arise out of marital breakdown or inadequate parenting. The jurisdiction may, however, by invoked jointly by happily married and responsible parents, as, for example, to restrain an adolescent child from pursuing an undesirable or potentially injurious relationship.

2 In this context, the parent with *de facto* custody of the children, whether or not this is in accordance with any existing order of the court.

3 Probation Rules 1965, Rule 18(2)(a); Home Office Circular 100/68; and Matrimonial Causes Rules 1977, Rule 95(1).
4 Matrimonial Causes Rules 1977, Rule 93(1).
5 Matrimonial Causes Rules 1977, Rule 95(3)(b).

CHAPTER 6: Matrimonial Supervision Orders

1 The interpretation of 'exceptional circumstances' and the implications of these provisions for the welfare officer in the preparation of his report are considered in chapter 5, page 117.
2 The application of this requirement, under Rule 93(1) of the Matrimonial Causes Rules 1973, is the same as in the context of the welfare enquiry, which is described in detail in chapter 5, page 118.
3 The choice of the appropriate supervising agency in this and other contexts is discussed on pages 137–9.
4 This problem is explored at length and with considerable illumination for those working in the sphere of divorce in the Finer Report: Report of the Committee on One Parent Families. Cmnd 5629, 1974, paras 7.1–7.41.
5 The nature of matrimonial supervision is such that an order made without a specific need first being identified or a minimum level of parental cooperation assured is unlikely to be very productive. It is therefore always desirable that judges contemplating supervision should adjourn the case for a welfare report, although they are not, of course, under any obligation to do so.

CHAPTER 7: Violent Families

1 Gayford, J. J., 'Wife battering: a preliminary survey of 100 cases', *British Medical Journal,* vol. i, 1975, pp. 194–7.
2 Brandon, S, 'Physical violence in the family: an overview', *Violence in the Family,* ed. Marie Borland, Manchester University Press, 1976, pp. 19–20.
3 Smith, Selwyn and Hanson, R, 'Social aspects of the battered baby syndrome', *British Medical Journal,* vol. iii, 1974, pp. 666–70.
4 Gayford, J. J., 'Wife battering: a preliminary survey of 100 cases', *British Medical Journal,* vol. i, 1975, pp. 194–7.
5 Brandon, S, 'Physical violence in the family', p. 21.
6 Ibid, p. 5.
7 Incestuous relationships between fathers and daughters are not uncommon in this multi-problem type of family. Recurrent sexual offences, often condoned by the mother, will sometimes accompany more conventional forms of family violence.

8 An amendment introduced by the Children Act 1975, under schedule 3, para 67.

9 The full list of relevant offences – basically ones involving physical or sexual assaults upon children – is set out in Schedule One of the Children and Young Persons Act 1933.

10 This amendment was introduced by the Children Act 1975, section 68.

11 The injunction is being considered here only in the context of actual physical violence. It does also offer a remedy where the health and well-being of the applicant and/or children of the family are at risk, although no act of violence has yet occurred.

12 There is a parallel here with Section 2(1)(e) of the Divorce Reform Act 1969, which first allowed divorce on the ground of five years' separation without consent. The late Baroness Summerskill described this clause as 'the Casanova's Charter', apparently envisaging the wholesale collapse of hitherto stable marriages, as middle-aged men abandoned their wives and families in favour of younger and more attractive women. In the event, the provision has achieved no more than was intended: the legal dissolution of marriages which continued in name only because of the refusal of the 'innocent' party to agree to a divorce.

It is reasonable to assume that this provision will only be used to protect unmarried women from the violence of their partners. Visions of predatory females attaching themselves to men for the sole purpose of parting them from their homes and property are surely more alarmist than sensible.

13 The objective of this Act, which is to bring the family law as administered by magistrates courts as far into line as is practicable with that embodied in the reformed law of divorce, is laudable within its prescribed limits. The measure of uniformity which has thus been obtained should not, however, be viewed as a viable alternative to the ultimate objective of establishing a single family jurisdiction, administered by a family court. The Act, however necessary in the short term, is really only a palliative measure; it does not seek to offer any solution to the many problems inherent in the continuing system of dual jurisdiction.

CHAPTER 8: Conclusions: The Future

1 Cases of particular difficulty may be referred to the Family Division by the county court, but these are too few in number to have any significant effect on this distribution.

2 Report of the Committee on One Parent Families, Cmnd 5629, 1974.

Guide to Further Reading

Borland, M. (Ed.) *Violence in the Family,* Manchester University Press, 1976.

Bromley, P. M. *Family Law,* Butterworth Press, 1976.

Dominian, J. *Family Breakdown,* Pelican, 1968.

Marriage Matters, HMSO, 1979.

A Better Way Out, The Law Society, 1979.

George, V. and Wilding, P. *Motherless Families,* Routledge and Kegan Paul, 1972.

Goldstein, J., Freud, A. and Solnit, A. J. *Beyond the Best Interests of the Child,* The Free Press/Macmillan Publishing Co. Inc., 1973.

Graham Hall, J. *The Case for Unified Family Courts,* National Council for One Parent Families, 1973.

Griew, E. and Bissett-Johnson, A. 'Supervision Orders in Matrimonial and Guardianship Cases', *Social Work Today,* vol. 6, no. 11, 4 September 1975.

'Welfare Reports', *Justice of the Peace,* 1 September 1979.

Hallett, K. *A Guide for Single Parents: Transactional Analysis for People in Crisis,* Celestial Arts, California, 1974.

'Bristol Courts Conciliation Service', Law Society's *Gazette,* 21 September 1980.

Marsden, D. *Mothers Alone,* Penguin, 1969.

McGregor, O. R. *Divorce in England,* Heinemann, 1957.

Putting Asunder: Divorce Law for Contemporary Society, SPCK, 1966.

Millard, D. A. 'The Welfare Task in Divorce Court Supervision Orders', *Justice of the Peace,* 3 February 1980.

Murcher, M. *Justice and Welfare in Divorce,* Sweet and Maxwell, 1980.

Pizzey, E. *Scream Quietly or the Neighbours will Hear,* Penguin, 1974.

'Conflicting Orders and the Child', *Justice of the Peace,* 16 December 1979.

Rowlands, P. *Saturday Parent,* George Allen and Unwin, 1980.

Wynn, M. *Fatherless Families,* Michael Joseph, 1970.

Index